# Doubt

Other books by Martin Israel include:

*Summons to Life* (Mowbray)
*Precarious Living* (Mowbray)
*Smouldering Fire* (Mowbray)
*The Spirit of Counsel* (Mowbray)
*Dark Victory* (Mowbray)

*Living Alone* (SPCK)
*The Pearl of Great Price* (SPCK)
*Night Thoughts* (SPCK)
*Life Eternal* (SPCK)
*The Quest for Wholeness* (Darton, Longman & Todd)
*Light on the Path* (Darton, Longman & Todd)
*The Pain That Heals* (Arthur James)

# Doubt

*The Way of Growth*

**Martin Israel**

MOWBRAY

**Mowbray**
A Cassell imprint
Wellington House, 125 Strand, London WC2R 0BB
PO Box 605, Herndon, VA 20172

First published 1997

British Library Cataloguing-in-Publication Data
A catalogue record for this book is available from the British Library.

ISBN 0-264-67435-9

Biblical quotations are mostly taken from The Revised English Bible,
© Oxford University Press and Cambridge University Press 1989

Typeset by ensystems, Saffron Walden, Essex
Printed and bound in Great Britain by J. W. Arrowsmith Ltd, Bristol

# Contents

# 1 The sunshine and the shadow

Man was made for Joy and Woe;
and when this we rightly know,
thro' the world we safely go.

Joy and Woe are woven fine,
a clothing for the soul divine.

This passage from William Blake's *Auguries of Innocence* reminds us of the light and its complementary darkness that compose the outer form as well as the inner essence of much of our lives on earth. Many of us are blessed with a cheerful disposition so that we can confront life's inevitable vicissitudes with relative composure. We know intuitively that all will be well on a deeper level with a degree of certainty greater even than that of Dame Julian of Norwich. In the type of person I am describing, the state of mind is joyfully intuitive and possibly a little too comfortable. Julian, as a great Christian mystic, knew that there was much disorder in the world but that God was nevertheless in control, and that his love would in due course fill the world with caring as a new order of relationships was born.

In other words, while a mystic could divine the great harmony that governed the cosmos that could not be disrupted by human action, even at its most destructive, they knew intuitively that human beings had to play their part in this transition from destructiveness to harmony. By contrast, the sanguine, or cheerful, type of person has only a limited insight into the world's workings and their personal relationships with the needs and controls which govern those workings of the Divine power that holds all material things in balance and harmonious rhythm. There is a higher order that controls the world's present chaos, but we ourselves are usually so concerned with our own troubles and ambitions that we are largely oblivious of our own immediate surroundings, let alone the larger universe that provides the key to the meaning of life and the way to eternity, an eternity revealed spontaneously to the mystic.

This type of person, as typified by Julian of Norwich and William Blake, has a natural gift from God enabling them to view eternal reality in the form of time and space in the present moment. So Blake would say in *Auguries of Innocence*:

> To see a World in a Grain of Sand,
> and a Heaven in a Wild Flower;
> Hold Infinity in the palm of your hand
> and Eternity in an hour.

A superficially cheerful type of individual seldom starts their worldly journey with much insight, as I have already intimated.

Living is mostly sunshine for them, especially in their youth when they are well cared for by a loving family. To be well nurtured as a young person used to be taken for granted, at least in polite and caring society and in the pages of the famous novels of the past era. Of course, the indignities of poverty rarely penetrated the consciousness of the rich and happy who had never seen the equivalent of fear, anger, envy, and deceit, while the tragedy of fatal disease was quietly brushed under the carpet of respectable life.

Life, however, has an invariable way of hitting back so as to disembarrass us of our illusions. If only things could always be as they were in our childhood, or after our conversion to religious faith or at the birth of our children (by far the loveliest of all babies!). This state of elation lasts for too short a period of time. Before we have had enough time really to enjoy our happiness, our triumph, the beauty of the world around us, an ominous pall of darkness rapidly approaches us and soon has us enfolded in its chilly grasp. In the darkness we begin to see the truth that illuminates the glory that for a time truly seemed to confront us: that all triumph is ephemeral dust, and death with dissolution is the common end of all that lives. In this respect, a biologist would accept

(a)  growth;
(b)  adaptation to external circumstances;
(c)  the development, on a mental level; and
(d)  the capacity to function on a more altruistic basis

as the features of life that have led to the perpetuation of the species, as far as we humans can judge this delicate issue. Is there any enduring principle to identify the living mass of tissue that we call a human, an animal, a plant, or even a parasitic worm? And if these do have a relevance peculiar to themselves, what does this relevance contribute to the world at large?

Why is the world occupied by so motley a throng of living forms ranging from the inspired human at their most glorious to the most pernicious bacteria that spread lethal disease? And yet again, is this lethal organism any more dangerous than the human who is mentally unbalanced, and who subsequently invades a classroom of children with a shotgun to aim indiscriminately and in uncontrollable rage at the children and in the process kills a considerable number of them? Is this act one of a criminal or of a psychotic maniac, and is the appropriate place of detention a mental hospital rather than a criminal cell? It all depends on whether one considers the person who committed this appalling action as severely mentally ill or as simply a hate-filled, inadequate human whose past history of loveless treatment and gross neglect has made them so envious of their contemporaries that they suddenly erupt in maddened fury as they consider their own misfortune. And what about the hate-filled individual who attains the leadership of a whole country, nation, or religious group: an individual typified by Adolf Hitler and many others in this century and earlier ones?

If one activity ought to bring humanity close to its divine roots, it is worship. Yet more cruelty and moral perversion has been carried out in the name of religion than in any other human activity. The God worshipped by so many people seems to be demonic rather than divine, and the more demonic that god shows himself or herself, the more votaries does he or she attract.

Voltaire parodied the indiscriminate optimism in *Candide* with the words of the over-enthusiastic Dr Pangloss, 'All is for the best in the best of possible worlds' ('Tout est pour le mieux dans le meilleur des mondes possibles'). The model for Dr Pangloss was the famous German philosopher Leibniz, but this comfortable view of the universe has been repeated in all ages among the complacent majority. Only those who are aware of the tragedy that overhangs all human relationships and separates the light from the darkness can learn that everything, no matter how remote it now seems, will have its day of reckoning, leaving an indelible stain of suffering as a memento of its advent.

In the wake of confusion and terror, disaster and despair we may catch a glimpse of how we really appear to ourselves, but the truth would be too cruel to tolerate for more than a very brief period of time. But how do we appear to others while in the grip of these terrible events, both internal and external? The truth is much less embarrassing. We do not appear very special to other people at all, because they tend to be centred on themselves almost exclusively. In other words, the world-view of most humans, including ourselves, is personally self-centred and socially parochial. When misfortune strikes, it at least has the cardinal virtue of elevating us beyond total self-absorption to a deeper awareness of the problems and tragedies of other people, so that we can by stages draw closer to the common membership we all share with creatures of the human race.

It is a disconcerting rule that prosperity tends to separate people whereas we all share in common poverty. The poverty of which I speak is not necessarily economic. It could quite as easily embrace social distinction, ill-health, or religious intolerance by a dominant group. The only wealth which alone is worth having is the wealth of the spirit which is, in fact, nothing else than the knowledge of God. This is the pearl of great price that Jesus spoke about in Matthew 13.46. A merchant looking for fine pearls found one of special value, so he went out and sold everything he had and bought it. To acquire this pearl one may have to part with so many earthly treasures that one is, indeed, reduced to a state of dire poverty. Only then may one be sufficiently cleansed of personal desire to be worthy to receive the priceless pearl which is a symbol of God's eternal presence as a cleansing, renewing love and wisdom. When we are full of our own wisdom, we are really empty of true understanding, because our own wisdom is an amalgam of worldly knowledge, personal prejudice, and ludicrous misinformation.

In this very familiar state of mind we are confused, bewildered, and deeply unhappy. Even if we staunchly believe that the world is going right generally, and for us personally, this response to the affairs of both the world generally, and ourselves specifically, is governed by our worldly situation and society around us, and by the state of our mind and soul. With regard to our psychological relationship to the outside world, there is, apart from obvious traumatic disturbance, the question of money that I have already touched upon; excess can be as debilitating as lack, inasmuch as it concentrates the awareness of the threat of poverty even when one's personal state of wealth is very impressive.

A neurotic personality depends on what is often called 'a heavy purse' to assuage their terror of penury. The main feature about financial security is that it cannot be attained by the type of neurotic personality I have described, as their state of anguish has often little to do with their financial position but is conveniently projected on to their money supply. Their problem is that of personal relationships: since they cannot deal adequately with themselves or their personal problems, they are most unlikely to relate well to anyone else either.

The most disconcerting experience of the descending

5

shadow of life tends to occur when we are still relatively young and inexperienced, and we accept people as a whole and the current views of the world's progress, because everyone and everything bears a reassuring smile, to the extent that we feel that we can trust both the world and its inhabitants as creatures of integrity. And then we are smitten with what is most appropriately called 'the Job experience', when, for no apparent reason, we are hit by a series of outrageous misfortunes which cause us to cry out in agony with apparently nobody to listen to, let alone be interested in answering, our pleas for enlightenment, or grant us relief. What have I done to deserve this tragedy? Why have my children entered criminal company with open eyes, despite the excellent education they have received? Why have I been the victim of persecution, whether personal, racial, national, or religious? I did not, to the best of my knowledge, choose any aberrant path or become involved in any subversive activity. To keep my hands and those of my family clean was a major concern of my life.

I was the product of a traditional, religious upbringing, and I was never at any time ashamed to bequeath this to my children. And yet, at the same time, I was never ignorant of the humiliating poverty and deep suffering of a large proportion of the population, both in my own native land and in the wider world. Moreover, I concerned myself with the welfare of these unfortunate people in the style of 1 John 4.20. 'If a man says, I love God, while at the same time hating his fellow Christian he is a liar. If he does not love a fellow Christian whom he has seen, he is incapable of loving God whom he has not seen.' In this political disaffection, we see the mystery of so much personal misfortune, and there is no source to afford an authoritative answer except to say that this is the way of the world, and we must come to terms with it as best we can. To be sure, the suffering coincident with ill-health may be subject to preventive measures, but as one group of diseases recedes into the background so others emerge almost automatically to replace them. Social injustice can be combated, by fiercer and yet at the same time more compassionate political action. But this very often leads to partisanship and greater discord than previously.

The French Revolution at the end of the eighteenth century inaugurated the ideals of liberty, equality, and fraternity upon a larger world, yet in the process did nothing to put an end to war and persecution. Indeed, the modern era of destructive nationalism dates from the French Revolution, which commenced with the flourish of the triumph of injustice overcome by the exertions of the common people against the combined might of the aristocracy and the professional army, and terminated with terrible violence against anyone suspected of reactionary views, which in fact meant views opposed to the power structure of those now governing the country. The destruction visited upon French culture was very considerable, and the country might have collapsed into total chaos had it not been for the emergence of a military genius, Napoleon Bonaparte, who unfortunately was less blessed in some other character traits, but who nevertheless carried through the work of the revolution until he himself was in due course defeated and there was a return to reactionary politics.

However, political justice was gradually established until in the twentieth century there was a great measure of co-operation between various countries and groups. Nevertheless, the emergence of Fascism and Nazism heralded the terrible persecution of the Jews and the humiliation of all who could not prove themselves to be of acceptable social or racial descent. The ending of the Second World War has given us all some temporary respite from widespread conflict. The present discord amongst so many nations and religious groups makes one wonder how long this blessed state of rest will endure. It is evident that the prescription of liberty, equality, and fraternity falls beautifully on the ears but does not descend like dew after a cool autumn evening. Water may come from on high but it is up to us to provide the right conditions for its condensation on the grass of our garden. We have to work with the garden to provide the most suitable atmospheric temperature, but we have to leave self

7

behind and work in weakness, in fear, and in great trepidation (1 Corinthians 2.3).

Meanwhile a very attractive political system was being devised in Germany and introduced into Eastern Europe in particular, where there was especially harsh poverty. It was called Socialism and, in its more extreme form, Communism. Its intellectual founder was Karl Marx. Two of his most celebrated sayings are 'The workers have nothing to lose in this revolution but their chains and have a world to gain. Workers of the world unite', and 'From each according to his abilities, to each according to his needs'. He also spoke of religion being the opium of the people, and his aim was the dictatorship of the proletariat.

State socialism still has something to offer in countries with a high standard of education, where an intelligent community can control the seductive invasion of socialistic power into its personal life, but the much more radical communistic system that ruined the lives of many in Russia and Eastern Europe has only recently been reversed, and has taken a much greater toll of the resources of these countries. China is still subject to the full blight of a socialistic dictatorship with little hope of any release until its people are inspired by the Holy Spirit to take matters into their own hands and follow the example of the West.

From these examples of health and social justice where the human has been blessed with a considerable degree of personal responsibility, we see that the result has been frankly disappointing because human expertise has far outstripped wisdom and self-control; only a severe reversal of fortune can affect this state of affairs. Balance is at the very heart of civilized living, and we tend to attain it late in the day. It is a paradox that we are regrettably short-lived and our lives full of trouble (Job 14.1), a frail mortal not worthy on one level of serious notice and yet at the same time little less than a god (Psalm 8.5–8). We grow from flimsiness to strength by doing our daily work with devotion to the world, while the obnoxious brilliance of the untempered mind learns to know its place and keep silent. By so doing it may at last know the true way of life.

At this point doubt comes to be seen as the authentic way of growth. What we want in life, or to be more candid, what we want to get out of life, may not be for our own ultimate good. Furthermore, we do not function as detached individuals, for we belong one to another as parts of one body (Ephesians 4.25). It could be that we are all parts of a universal plan, insignificant as we individuals would appear to be. On the other hand, we may believe that our work is so important that it is a crying shame that it is unceremoniously thwarted by misfortune; and what, in any case, is this alleged plan? Is any tangible power in a conceivable way concerned with our little, private world, or is this merely a childish illusion? This is how most of us come as near to our concept of God as we can comprehend but what a childishly self-centred view it embraces!

There is quite interestingly a deeper sense of composure when we know pain and have to accommodate it, than when all is apparently progressing well, but we are in a state of suffused fear in anticipation of later trouble. In this respect, the temptation to compromise with moral ambiguities is the one truly demonic component of our earthly life. It has to be confronted directly and dealt with speedily. This is done by ardent prayer, by which I mean lifting up our consciousness to the All Highest, whom we know by intuition and not by intellectual speculation. It is at this point that we may glimpse God, for in such company all worldly distractions simply fall away from us.

In this ego-less realm we are in truth in the Divine company, and can now offer ourselves without restriction to the Divine Grace, which is a really satisfactory way of identifying God, as opposed to a worldly personage. It is evident that the sunshine period of life, pleasant though it may be, has to be outgrown if we are to use our own God-given powers for our own benefit and that of the world around us. Growth is an essential feature of the process of life, while a failure to progress is an ominous sign of atrophy and a movement towards decline and death.

Life is always interesting, sometimes thrilling, not infrequently breathtaking, but never without some interest that drives one on to despair at humanity and at one's own ability too. The despair that humanity inculcates in us is due to its lack of imagination in personal relationships, and it is the hope that springs eternal in the human breast that Alexander Pope wrote about in his *Essay on Man* (I, 95), that related to humanity's capacity to repent and confess its sins in childlike honesty.

Humanity's great dilemma is to learn how to build on past experience so that the same suffering may truly be obviated, and a new way of life may be embarked upon. It is the repeated failure of humanity to learn in the depths of its soul the lessons of a previous generation and not to commit the same errors, time and time again, that are the cause of its repeated suffering. A particular error may be registered so that it is not readily repeated, but then a not very different mistake is made under a different guise. The same trail of consequences will inevitably follow.

From this sequence of events it becomes apparent that most of us simply do not grow and act as responsible adults. We do not really know ourselves, as people, and live under a cloud of illusion. Disaster cuts the ground from under our feet, and then we may begin to see the truth which is alleged to set us free in John 8.32. It certainly does free us from the illusion of independence, for we are all parts of the one body (Ephesians 4.25). Once the monumental significance of this truth seeps into the deepest recesses of our mind, we begin to assert our private mind less vociferously and become more open to other people's opinions on a considerable range of topics, in so doing, growing in personal knowledge as opposed to mere individual prejudice.

Doubt is a maturing process, for in its cold embrace we have left comfort far behind us. It is cold, ruthless, and a hard task-master. It also makes us an uncomfortable bedfellow for many a friend who previously may have valued our advice no less than our company. But it also has its rewards, for it sets us on the path that leads to truth. Certainty cannot tolerate the cold breath of doubt, because in its presence all that is false and tainted shrinks in dismay, but it does not shrink from the doubt nearly so much as from its own corrupt self. We grow as we depend progressively less not on human company or worldly knowledge, but on illusion. This may be sensory or delusive, so as to be deceptive and unreal. Therefore, it can be said that doubt illuminates certainty and strengthens it to withstand the forces of destruction that threaten our world day by day.

It is amazing how refreshing a period of chilling doubt can be in making us strong enough to withstand the Job experience or even our own Gethsemane in the company of the discredited Christ himself before he rose from the dead.

# 2 The Job experience

There lived in the land of Uz a man of blameless and upright life named Job who feared God and set his face against wrongdoing. He had seven sons and three daughters and he owned a multitude of cattle as well as many slaves. So he was the greatest man in all the East. His sons used to meet together and gave each in turn a banquet in his own house and they would send and invite their three sisters to eat and drink with them. Then when the round of banquets was over, Job would send for his children and sanctify them, rising early in the morning and sacrificing a whole offering for each of them, for he thought that they might somehow have sinned against God and committed blasphemy in their hearts. This Job did regularly.

The first chapter of this immortal story moves on to the Court of Heaven, where the various members took their place in the presence of the Lord and the adversary, Satan, was there among them. And the Lord asked him where he had been. 'Ranging over the earth from end to end' was the reply. And the Lord then asked him if he had considered his servant Job, for he would find no one like him on earth, a man of blameless and upright life who preferred God and set his face against wrongdoing. At this point the adversary becomes much more malicious.

Has not Job good reason to be God-fearing, have you not hedged him round on every side with your protection, him and his family and all his possessions? Whatever he does, you have blessed and everywhere his herds have increased beyond measure. But just stretch out your hand and touch all that he has, and see if he will not curse you to your face.

The Lord at once delivered all that Job possessed into the hands of the adversary with the proviso that Job himself should not be touched. And so on the day when Job's sons and daughters were eating and drinking at their eldest brother's house a messenger came to Job to tell him that a host of Sabaeans had swooped down and carried off the flocks and donkeys after killing the herdsman. Almost simultaneously another messenger arrived and said that God's fire had lashed down from heaven striking the sheep and shepherds and burning them up; he alone was preserved to bring the news. While he was still speaking, another arrived and said 'The Chaldeans, three bands of them, have made a raid on the camels and carried them off, after putting those who tended them to the sword. Only I have escaped to bring you the news.' As he spoke yet another messenger arrived and said 'Your sons and daughters were eating and drinking in their eldest brother's house when suddenly a whirlwind swept across the desert and struck the four corners of the house which fell on the young people and they are dead. Only I have escaped to bring you the news.' At this Job stood up, tore his cloak, shaved his head and threw himself prostrate on the ground, saying: 'Naked I came from the womb, naked I shall return whence I came. The Lord gives and the Lord takes away; blessed be the name of the Lord.' Throughout all this Job did not sin nor did he ascribe any fault to God (Job 1 – 3).

Once again God points out Job's sanctity to Satan in the second chapter only to be met with the challenge that when Job's health is also destroyed, then he will most certainly curse God to his face. And so God puts Job into Satan's fell clutches with the sole proviso that his life is spared. Job becomes afflicted with a most terrible skin disease so that his wife challenges him not to hold fast to his integrity but rather to curse God and die (Job 2.9). Job compares her advice to that of any impious woman, making the important observation that if we accept good from God shall we not accept evil also? Throughout all this Job does not utter one sinful word. Then Job's three friends, Eliphaz from Teman, Bildad from Shuha and Zophar from Naama, having heard of all the calamities that had overtaken Job, come to comfort and condole with him. But Job in chapter 3 first curses the day that he was born. He asks why a man should be born to wander blindly hedged about by God on every side; sighing for him is his only food, and every terror that haunted him has caught up with him. What he dreaded has overtaken him and there is no peace of mind, no quiet for him. Trouble comes, but he has no rest.

In the first cycle of his speeches Eliphaz takes over chapters 4 and 5. He first gently chides Job for his impatience, for his piety ought to give him absolute faith in help. Have the innocent ever perished? But he has seen those who plough mischief and sow trouble reap no other harvest, perishing at the blast of God and being shrivelled by the breath of his nostrils. Eliphaz tells of a word that came to him stealthily in the anxious visions of the night. A formless presence that filled him with fear. He heard a voice murmur 'Can a human being be righteous before God if he mistrusts his own servants and finds his messengers (the angels) at fault, how much more those who live in houses on earth whose foundations are in dust; how much more shall they perish unheeded together, only to die without finding wisdom'. Eliphaz counsels Job to make a direct appeal to God who does great and unsearchable things, who may rebuke one only to show his greater capacity to heal afterwards.

All this contains some truth, but why the pain in the first place in the case of a blameless, virtuous man? Eliphaz does mention the disciplinary value of painful experience but does this really apply in Job's case? Certainly, it washes over poor Job like water off a duck's back, for in chapters 6 and 7 he roundly declares his innocence. He is convinced that death is close at hand. He asks 'Does not every mortal have hard service on earth and are not his days like those of a hired labourer, like those of a slave kept waiting for his wages?' One might remember the days of radiant prosperity that had preceded Job's catastrophe, but our memories are short-lived. Job's final lament is especially moving. 'What is man that you make much of him and turn your thoughts towards him, only to punish him morning after morning, or to test him every hour of the day?' Job asks God if he will not look back away from him for a single instant so that he can at least swallow his saliva. or if he has indeed sinned, what harm has he done God? Surely he will lie in the dust of the grave. You may seek him, but he shall be no more.

Bildad and Zophar repeat the basic assertions of God or God's state of love and justice, and that it is right for Job to bear his present distress for further instruction and future understanding. But Job is unmoved by all this comfortable rhetoric pouring forth from those who are full of knowledge but illuminated by a minimum of experience that alone makes this knowledge credible. This is indeed the crucial difference between knowledge and wisdom. The first is learned from reading books and listening to various authorities, whereas the second proceeds directly from the experience of life itself. Wisdom alone can teach and test the veracity of the human heart and the truth of another person's experience of life. Wisdom is the supreme working of the Holy Spirit in the human soul, and it is easily overlaid by the glib assurance of various plausible 'experts'.

The three friends praise God's magnificence and glory, and all affirm that Job's suffering must be due to great sinfulness, a charge that Job absolutely repudiates. In chapter 28 there is a marvellous Wisdom Poem that is not directly connected with the main theme of Job's suffering. But has Job in fact been guilty of any wrongdoing? On the surface, the answer must be in the negative. However, chapters 29 to 31 reveal a weakness to the astute reader.

> If only I could go back to the old days, to the times when God was watching over me, when his lamp shone over my head and by its light I walked through the darkness. If I could be as in the days of my prime when God protected my home. when the Almighty was still there at my side, when my servants stood around me while my paths flowed with milk and the rocks poured forth streams of oil for me.

Then follows a most revealing passage.

When I went out of my gate, up to the town to take my seat in the public square, young men saw me and kept back out of sight. Old men rose to their feet. Men in authority broke off their talk and put their hands over their lips, the voices of the nobles died away and every man held his tongue. They listened expectantly, and waited in silence to my counsels; after I had spoken nobody spoke again. My words fell gently upon them. They waited for me as for rain, open-mouthed as for spring showers. When I smiled on them, they took heart; when my face lit up, they lost their gloomy looks. I presided over them, planning their course like a king encamped with his troops; like one who comforts mourners.

Job continues in this self-congratulatory style in chapters 29 to 31. 'Whoever heard me, spoke favourably of me, and those who saw me bore witness to my merit, how I saved the poor who appealed for help, and the fatherless and him who had no protector.' The person threatened with ruin blessed Job and he made the widow's heart sing for joy. He put on righteousness as a garment; justice, like a cloak and turban, adorned him. He was eyes to the blind and feet to the lame. He was a father to the needy and took up the stranger's cause. He broke the fangs of the miscreant and wrested the prey from his teeth. He thought he would die with unimpaired powers and days uncounted as the grains of sand, with his roots spreading out to the water and the dew lying on his branches.

If one considers Job's self-congratulation seriously and sympathetically, it is evident how hard it is not to look for a reward for some admirable past action. We are brought up with the expectation but with varying degrees of disapproval if we fail to meet the mark. This approach has a degree of justice, and if there were a greater degree of training for the young in basic issues of morality, much suffering would certainly be averted; surely the consequence of bad behaviour is alienation from society until amends have been sincerely made, and the humiliation causes the individual to respect other people's welfare as well as their own, giving the

possibility of goodness and happiness. But if the reward for
anti-social behaviour is suffering ranging from ostracism to
imprisonment, is the reward for the good person spontaneously glorious? Does such a person attain national
eminence, social importance, great wealth, or the esteem of
those who are considered authorities on spiritual themes?

The honest answer is 'generally, in due course, if ever at
all'. When the great wrath of God in Israel was confronted
in a state of general confusion, whether personal, religious,
or national, the advice of the great prophets was assiduously
sought during the period of natural emergency, but their
advice was nearly always forgotten when a state of equilib-
rium had been attained once more.

In other words, the reward for decent spiritual living is
little more than material stability during a period of national
tranquillity, remembering, after the manner of Job, the
evanescent value of money in a world of turmoil. There is
absolutely no evidence that good fortune on the money
markets is in any way related to the morality of the individual
investor, nor is their state of health automatically less sound
than that of those whose way of life is dedicated to the
welfare of the sick and the bereaved. There is, in other words,
apparently nothing to be gained, at least on a purely worldly
level, by a virtuous, compassionate way of life, despite the
frequent exhortations in the Old Testament and the
Apocrypha.

Consider the counsel in the book of Tobit.

> Distribute alms from what you possess and never with a
> grudging eye. Do not turn your face away from any poor man,
> and God will not turn away his face from you. Let your
> almsgiving match your means. If you have little, do not be
> ashamed to give the little you can afford; you will be laying up
> sound insurance against the day of adversity. Almsgiving pre-
> serves the giver from death and keeps him from going down into
> darkness. All who give alms are making an offering acceptable
> to the Most High. (Tobit 4.7–11)

In the Acts of the Apostles the generosity of Barnabas is
especially praised. The whole company of believers was

united in heart and soul. Not one of them would claim any of his possessions as his own. Everything was held in common. With great power the apostles bore witness to the resurrection of the Lord Jesus and all were held in great esteem. There was never a needy person among them, for all who had property in land or houses would sell it, bring the proceeds of the sale and lay it at the feet of the apostles to be distributed to any who were in need.

For instance Joseph, surnamed by the apostles Barnabas, which means 'son of encouragement' (and a Levite Cypriot), sold an estate which he owned and he brought the money and laid it at the apostles' feet. The same Barnabas was, as we know subsequently, to befriend Paul and to make him acceptable to the apostles because his notoriety as a persecutor of the earliest Christians, especially Stephen, made them shrink from him in fear. That such a person should now come to be on their side, heart and soul, seemed truly incredible.

The presence of the living Christ among them brought the apostles true contentment and peace which had been hard to attain in the midst of severe persecution – and this is what the Job experience is especially here to teach us – that truly nothing belongs to us, not even our own children, and that everything and every occurrence in our lives are here to open our eyes to the reality of the self, and from the self to all other selves also. This is primarily human but stretches through the animal and vegetable kingdoms also. We see how small our place is in the Divine scheme, and the more we can let go of thoughts of ownership, the more we can concern ourselves with life in its wholeness.

In the various discourses that shed light on the characters of the participants as the book of Job proceeds, there is an unheralded intrusion of a fourth person, Elihu. He is an impetuous young man who is infuriated on behalf of God's honour, for Job had made himself out to be more righteous than God. His three friends had found no answer to Job, since only God appeared to be acting wrongly. In a long-winded discourse in chapters 32 to 37 Elihu praises the absolute strength and justice of God and, by contrast, the weakness of the leading characters. It is not in the nature of God to bring about suffering like Job's terrible ordeal so close to death unless that person was guilty of great sin and showed no sign of repentance. Therefore, sin is, after all, the cause of Job's travail, and the sooner he ceases to adopt the self-righteous pose and face the facts of his previous life squarely, the more speedily will his relief come. Little is added by this discourse to the observations already made by the three friends and also by Job himself.

The one evident observation is that the human being does not understand the inner workings of providence or the outer desires of their own heart. They want everything to be as pleasant as possible but they are not prepared to put themselves out to attain this goal, except perhaps by the exploitation of their fellow creatures with little concern for their individual welfare. In chapter 38 God himself makes his appearance in the traditional form of a supernatural power, issuing forth from the tempest. He puts Job to the test in the next four chapters, stressing his creative power in what he has achieved from the whole natural order. Has Job any understanding of how the earth's foundations were laid, or who fixed its dimensions? So the questioning continues until the various animal species are also described: this lesson in natural history is absolutely fascinating but has little to do with Job's suffering except peripherally in respect of God's power and magnificence towards his creatures. But what about Job, the most intelligent and sensitive of all of them?

At any rate, Job's questions are satisfied by his encountering God directly. He says 'I know that you can do all things, and that no purpose is beyond you. You ask: "Who is this obscuring counsel, yet lacking knowledge?" But I have spoken of things which I have not understood, things too wonderful for me to know.' In this confession of Job (42.1–6), he at least acknowledges that while he previously had known of God only by report, now he can see him with his own eyes and he repents in dust and ashes (for his doubt). The end of the chapter has a fairy-tale atmosphere with Job interceding for his friends because they did not give the right doctrine about God. At the same time Job's possessions are restored to him, his relatives come and feast at his home, comforting and consoling him for all his past afflictions, and each giving him a sheep and a gold ring. He also has seven sons and three daughters more beautiful than any other women in the world, and Job gave them an inheritance with their brothers. Job lived another 140 years after all this.

When one considers the whole narrative, one is aware of an aspect of anti-climax, inasmuch as the harrowing part of the ordeal is magically reversed, Job is instructed in the creative ways of God, and then has a fortune bestowed on him. No explanation of this dramatic change in his fortunes is supplied. Since Job is fundamentally a decent God-fearing man, even if some of that fear has a self-centred basis, the one message that comes through loud and clear is the unpredictable nature of our life on earth, and that we dare not bargain with the powers that be for our survival, let alone our certain good fortune. Job's fortitude is tested to prove his sincerity of heart, and he is extremely fortunate to be left alive at the end of his ordeal.

But how many victims of the most terrible persecutions that have disgraced human society throughout the centuries have gone unsung to their graves? If we are wise, we do tend to learn something from the story of Job – not that piety will deliver us from evil, so much as that a keen regard for common decency will provide us with the strength of character to overcome evil. In other words, that strength comes from within although of course it has its primary origin from God. We are, however, ill-advised to depend on divine assistance if we are not prepared to play our part also. This is the full nature of human responsibility, and if we were to abrogate it, our lives would be immeasurably impoverished. With these thoughts in mind we need not be over-solicitous about the fate of Job, terrible as some of his pains seem to have been.

Living contains within it the seeds of suffering, as no doubt Job knew long before his dramatic fall into penury and ill-health, to say nothing of his terrible bereavement of all his family apart from his cantankerous wife. It is probable, if we take the final chapter of the book literally, that his fine, fresh, young family was born of a younger, much more pleasant wife.

The full thrust of the Job experience is liable to afflict any of us when all our customary ways of life are suddenly and summarily shattered by some intervening event, and stark reality faces us. The precipitating factor may be an incurable disease, the death of a close friend, the failure of a venture on which we had pinned all our hopes and prayers, or the simple betrayal of trust by someone we sincerely believed to be honest in their dealings. In all these instances and many others too we have been seriously let down and our hopes, at least temporarily, are dashed. The pain of much of life is related to its apparent meaninglessness. Young people with much promise ahead of them are suddenly stricken by incapacitating illnesses that thwart their creativity and make chronic invalids of them. There is also the tragedy of progressive mental disease, notably schizophrenia, cutting short the full blossoming of a young person's life, so that they may need institutional care whereas they would once have enjoyed an enviable life with their friends.

Life on earth certainly reminds us of the frailty of the physical body, and also the instability of the emotional life that focuses both on the brain and on past experiences we have had to endure in the midst of a society that is seldom favourably disposed to the needs of its especially sensitive members.

It is not surprising that the doubt at the time poor unfortunate Job had to bear is a natural part of human experience. What is the meaning of it all? Why do our personal experiences run so obviously counter to the teaching of the Church? Why was the counsel of Job's three friends not only futile but also infuriatingly smug, a criticism, incidentally, of much teaching from 'religious' people? Why is there so seldom anyone to listen to our questions on a higher level of understanding or compassion? Even Job did not receive this courtesy. He was simply given a view of God's magnificence and restored to health and good fortune, but he received no explanation of his suffering. We have at least been given the answer to his problem – the contest between the forces of darkness and light with the person of Job acting as the object of a celestial tug-of-war between them. But he personally knew nothing of all this in his own battle for survival. Is this in fact the purpose of individual suffering? Is this the purpose of doubt in the growth to maturity of any individual?

It seems clear to me that agnosticism, the capacity to accommodate doubt where there is no cut-or-dried answer to any final question, is absolutely necessary if we are to come within any hailing distance of the truth. In fact, it is doubtful if we can ever know absolute truth in our present state of moral and spiritual development. But it is in the nature of truth always to recede from us, the more intimately we venture into its recesses. Doubt with experience can be seen as a denial of an absolute answer to any personal, communal, or universal problem.

On the other hand, it is sensible to trust the advice of an acknowledged specialist in a worldly discipline, like medical practice, accountancy, or the law. Then one would be closer to the truth than if one were to trust in one's own intuition or that of an unskilled practitioner. In worldly transactions of this type, doubt should be largely assuaged by confidence in the ability of the practitioner who is being consulted. Their reputation should afford as much trust as any of us could reasonably demand.

In the world of the spirit we are right to assess people by the impact they make upon our intuition, but in the end it is their work that counts. 'Truly I tell you: anything you did for one of my brothers here, however insignificant, you did for me' (Matthew 25.40). This must be placed in opposition to 1 Corinthians 13.3: 'I may give all I possess to the needy, I may give my body to be burnt, but if I have no love, I gain nothing by it.' Therefore, love is shown by works as well as by our inner attitude to people.

# 3 Doubt and self-knowledge

There are two different categories of humans in terms of Jungian typology: the introvert and the extrovert. The mind of the introvert tends to turn inward on itself, the state called introspection, whereas the extrovert has the outer world as their focus of attention. The way of the extrovert is assuredly more relaxing because they can enjoy the world generally without bearing some of its implications with the same gravity that is more customary among introverts. Thus following 1 Corinthians 15.32, they can say of life and its termination 'Let us eat and drink, for tomorrow we die'. This quotation is typical of the extrovert attitude to life and death, for it concerns itself chiefly with the immediate present, and has little concern for the things of eternity. The extrovert would be more likely to reject spiritual matters as being irrelevant to their and the world's present needs, and in any case completely unproven and a mere sell-out to the forces of superstition and fear. What is immediately demonstrable and therefore provable would alone fulfil their satisfaction.

Such a view of life is by no means totally unacceptable or absolutely incompatible with their spiritual vision (as far as this can accommodate spiritual forces among the various unseen circumstances that would appear to govern any person's life), and it learns to embrace a degree of sensibility to the needs of other people also, inasmuch as the extrovert's awareness starts to turn away from their own sole concerns to those of other people, which after all is the basis of civilized, communal living. The problem associated with a typical extrovert is a certain lack of imagination. They find it hard to enter into the life of another person because their own inner life is so much a closed book to them. They tend to ride roughshod over the feelings of other people, not so much through hostility or disdain as through pure insensitivity, which is an almost inevitable result of not having had the experience of being inwardly bruised through the unkindness of other people in their earlier years, when their own feelings were especially tender.

The introvert, by contrast, knows at an early stage of their life what it feels like to be inwardly hurt. Their self-confidence, or self-esteem if they have been the butt of the ridicule or cruelty of their teachers or peers, is easily shaken, and they cannot take their own safety, let alone invulnerability, for granted.

I do not believe that this negative response to the challenges of life is simply a reaction to past experience, for character is also moulded by genetic influences, the health of the person and their family background, and spiritual factors which cannot be glimpsed by outsiders until they have gained some insight into their own character in terms of strength and weakness. The introvert starts life at a considerable social disadvantage for which they may overcompensate by an acute awareness of their relationship with those around them. They may feel deeply, at first in a self-centred way in terms of what others think about them, but later they can become increasingly concerned about the lives and welfare of numerous other people. All this devolves upon them as they begin to comprehend their call to universal service, learning to feel that we all belong to one another as parts of one body (Ephesians 4.25).

The path of the introvert is therefore more distinctly solitary than that of the extrovert. It has much less social entertainment at the end of the day, but its rewards are correspondingly more impressive. Most of the innovatory geniuses of the world come from within its borders.

In fact, what we learn about ourselves comes basically from two sources. First of all, there are our relationships with those around us who impinge immediately upon us, whether positively or negatively. The other source of self-knowledge is the effect of life's various vicissitudes, whether positive or negative. Positive vicissitudes include material success, happy relationships, and good health, whereas negative vicissitudes comprise such emotional shocks as disappointment, bereavement, ill-health, and betrayal, to name but a few. The introvert learns to come to terms with life's debris no less than its beauty at an early age. The extrovert seems to have no difficulty in shutting their eyes to life's more sordid aspects and living in a cloud of optimism. They are confident about their own capacity to win through despite the disillusionment of much of life's experience. Indeed, their life is a splendidly adventurous one, and a very important property shared in common between extroverts and introverts is courage, a most admirable quality which consists in boldness to hold fast to one's convictions despite all discord and to act upon them.

The tenacity and strength of one's belief, even to death if need be, are typical of courage. It may be ill advised, but it cannot be accused of the frailty of doubt. There is, however, a distinct difference between the extrovert's and the introvert's courage; the former has little concern for their life or reputation in people's eyes, acting not so much out of humility but as a gesture of pure, unsought bravery, or in its less admirable form, defiance or foolhardiness, whereas the introvert's courage is keenly concerned with other people's attitudes and views on their own past life and general reputation.

They tend to have rather less personal and social ease, so that their particular type of courage takes the form of putting on a brave face in the company of people whom they do not know socially, especially those who are renowned for some particular feat or quality. In this they show, at least to themselves, that they too have something to offer and are not merely nonentities. If only we were all aware of how little other people cared about us, our social background, and even our personal appearance (within, of course, the limits of respectability), a great deal of anxiety would drop from us very rapidly, but we, especially the introverts among our number, are often so imprisoned in our own illusion of inferiority, which is in fact a state of feeling ill at ease in our social environment, that we dare not drop the mask of convention and begin to become authentically ourselves. This is the paralysing aspect of doubt that is frequently unknown to the extrovert, who in turn follows their own way oblivious of the effect they are having on other people.

Should doubt in fact have this effect in the living of our lives? And if it should, what are the criteria we should be applying to ascertain whether it is functioning properly and not deleteriously? During much of our time there seems to be scant reason to doubt either our way of life or our motives; introspection, the way of the introvert, can easily be exaggerated to the extent that all initiative is suffocated, as the various aspects influencing the course of an enterprise begin to form the basis of an interminable debate.

We are always wise to listen to various views, even if they strike no note of recognition in our own mind, for by this open discussion we are more likely to come to the truth about a private matter. When we are sure that our own approach is without fault and our own opinions are clearly in the right, this is the time to watch out and keep our eyes fixed on the present moment, for here lies the stone on which we will be especially liable to trip and sustain a severe fracture of faith. What I am saying is this: the important aspect of doubt that shows itself in our lives is related not only to our character but also as a response to the various challenging experiences in our lives.

When a sequence of misfortunes afflicts our life, it may well be that the cause is related to our own *insouciance*. Sometimes a severe emotional response can complicate personal issues of one type or another that have gone wrong. On occasion there may be a psychic rebound to add its burden to the emotional one. To some of us this is pure unsubstantiated superstition, but others with a more sensitive temperament tend to be more tolerant to this type of approach.

Self-knowledge is frequently lacking in the extrovert, who considers that their customary state of awareness is clearly identical with things as they really are, and their usual feelings are a precise summary of their inner life, even if the tenor varies according to the present circumstances. To many extroverts the very concept of 'inner life' may be incomprehensible, for after all there is only one life and this is identical with the sum total of the individual's present awareness. With such a limited understanding, there can be only a very restricted view of the feelings, indeed the life, of another person. Obviously, such a confined understanding of the nature of a person is inadequate because it evades vast tracts of personality that are peculiar to a particular individual, whilst tending to place people into various idiosyncratic categories that may bear little resemblance to those that have been formulated by specialists in psychological typology.

An extrovert would tend to be nonplussed and sometimes a little irritated also by the failure of those who they believe can make their mark in the world of endeavour and worldly success, and would tend to attribute the failure to produce anything worthwhile by intellectually and artistically sterile people to their general ineptitude, coupled with a rampant laziness. This harsh judgement is related to the absence of empathy, and is not a product of hard-heartedness so much as a general insensitivity to other people's fears and feelings, and their often desperate prayers to be shown the light of truth in the dark fog that clouds so much of the atmosphere in which they live their lives on earth. It is characteristic of the extrovert's awareness that there is a general satisfaction in their lifestyle and that of their family, at least when it is young. There may be material problems with their collective well-being, but once these threatening factors have been banished by direct action, doubt is soon dispelled and a new *status quo* is attained. Indeed, an extrovert's life can be extremely pleasant among strangers, but in due course its orderly progress is liable to be shattered by tragedy or disaster of one type or another.

The confidence of the extrovert is seen in the introvert's way of life also, but here there is less naïve trust in their own capacity and a greater respect for the forces of the universe that sustain all our lives. I prefer to use this term rather than the word God because the concept is open to so many doubtful assumptions. The question about whether these universal powers are totally beneficial or not was considered in the second chapter in relationship to Job's suffering, and we came to the conclusion that their great benefit lay in making humans more able to confront their challenge without flinching, stronger, and more serviceable to their fellows by virtue of their own experience. Therefore, there is only one ultimate source of courage, but whereas an extrovert would see it as intrinsic to their own personality, the introvert would have a wider, more universal approach with special reference to a power far beyond their own scope.

A well-known poem by Arthur Hugh Clough (1819–61) gives an eloquent approach to doubt in the universal process of life and death in the world.

Say not the struggle naught availeth,
The labour and the wounds are vain,
The enemy faints not, nor faileth,
And as things have been, they remain.

If hopes were dupes, fears may be liars;
It may be, in yon smoke concealed,
Your comrades chase e'en now the flyers,
And, but for you, possess the field.

For while the tired waves, vainly breaking,
Seem here no painful inch to gain,
Far back through creeks and inlets making
Comes silent, flooding in, the main.

And not by eastern windows only,
When daylight comes, comes in the light,
In front the sun climbs slow, how slowly,
But westward, look, the land is bright.

This poem (called 'Say Not the Struggle Naught Availeth') is a most eloquent expression of the necessity of doubt in the experience of self-knowledge. When we believe we have little to offer the world or our small patch in it, then we may discover our own unique, if humble, place in the scheme of life. The reason for this lies in the uniqueness of our own personality, which, incidentally, includes much more than merely a question of extroversion versus introversion. Doubt is also important in bringing us back down to reality if we tend to have too high an opinion of our own abilities. Nobody enjoys being criticized because of the deflating effect on their personality. By nature, there are few of us who actually see ourselves realistically; while some are immersed in feelings of inferiority when compared with people whom they know, others believe that they are naturally gifted and form a superior élite. In fact, all these distinctions are vain. What is important is that we should actualize our own gifts for the use of the community and not to our own advantage. This is the way of illusion, as our own personal advantage soon fades before the winds of disaster when we are confronted by market forces far beyond our manipulation.

I have complete assurance that doubt is invaluable in helping us to become a mature person, maturing in this context being completeness in natural development with fully developed powers of body and mind. But the question that was asked earlier on in the chapter remains: What criteria should we use to find out whether doubt is functioning properly or deleteriously in our lives? If doubt functions in a deleterious way, it becomes injurious to our well-being, interfering with the normal performance of our work, even to the extent of producing a fear within us that we may be the victims of accidents or violence if we pursue the normal course of our lives. There is a subtle difference between doubt and uncertainty. Though doubt is frequently defined as a feeling of uncertainty, an undecided state of mind, and an inclination to disbelieve what other people say or teach, the kernel of doubt lies buried in the depth of the mind, called the unconscious, and is open to exposure by any fresh experience that causes the person to recall wounding events of long ago, including those of childhood and adolescence. The memory of these causes a person to respond painfully to a past era of their lives. It may be advisable to undergo psychotherapy in order to reveal masking material in the unconscious that is preventing the individual seeing themself more significantly as a universal being, no longer restricted by barriers of race, religion, or nationality. An alternative way is one of counselling with a space for prayer, confession and absolution. This more gentle approach will sometimes be especially effective for one obsessed by doubts of a spiritual nature.

The word 'spiritual' in this context appertains to the loving God of religion and all that relates directly to him. There is much more to God than merely a reassuring presence which makes us feel warm and comfortable. Indeed, the very presence of God is the greatest of all mysteries, and cannot be taken for granted by anyone attempting to penetrate the heart of doubt: after all, if we could take the Divine Presence and initiative for granted, the teeth would be largely extracted from doubt, which would remain little more than a small awareness of transient, individual inadequacy. But, of course, even this statement requires some modification. Job learnt there was a cruel, unpredictable streak in God's relationship with his creatures. We need not be anchored in his own story and even reflect on the natural tragedies that punctuate the world's history from age to age.

I am not including in these events the various horrors that have followed human cruelty which are not directly attributable to Divine action. The human being has been given the power of a god, which can be defined as a creature blessed with the gift of free will. In our world we are unique in this respect. Psalm 82 has much to say about the subject.

God takes his place in the court of heaven
to pronounce judgement among the gods;
'How much longer will you judge unjustly and favour the
    wicked?

Uphold the cause of the weak and the fatherless,
and see right done to the afflicted and destitute.
Rescue the weak and the needy,
and save them from the clutches of the wicked.'
But these gods know nothing and understand nothing,
they walk about in darkness;
meanwhile, earth's foundations are all giving way.
This is my sentence:
'Though you are gods, all sons of the Most High,
yet you shall die as mortals die,
and fall as any prince does.'
God, arise and judge the earth,
for all the nations are yours.

When Jesus is attacked by the Jews for claiming to be God, he quotes the last part of the Psalm to justify his claim, teaching that it is those to whom God's words come who are called gods.

The question remains, of course, whether his godhead is similar to that of any other human or of a distinctly more holy type due to his consecration by the Father (John 10.34–38). It was this claim that infuriated the Jews so much that they desired to stone him. If we read the Gospel in the spirit of reasonable doubt, we too might raise our eyebrows at Jesus' claims during his teaching ministry before he was tested at the time of his death, and here we have to come to our own conclusions. Certainly, this particular claim attributed to Jesus is peculiar to John's Gospel and is not found in the same way in any of the other three preceding synoptic ones. But these three Gospels – Matthew, Mark, and Luke – had a very different style and content to the fourth, which is based on the manifestation of Christ's glory from the earliest miracles to the resurrection. But how much we can accept of all this narrative depends ultimately on our own discernment. Doubt is certainly a hard task-master, but when we have come to grips with this challenge, we emerge as stronger, more independent individuals. We are more capable of making our own decisions and acting on them with strength and determination. We are able to face the worst in a situation, we can relax and work our way forward with faith and courage. The cleansing effect of doubt wipes away all illusion from us, and then we can begin to do our work with ease and inner joy.

My own opinion is that Jesus did indeed show many exceptional spiritual gifts, but that his followers have often failed notably to do much more than indulge in sectarian warfare, while the teaching has flown out of the window. Charismatic spiritual leaders can easily let their flock depend almost entirely on their gifts, while doubt is abandoned in the interests of respect and homage. This gullibility can have a baneful effect on the lives of both the leader and their flock. The leader can be so seduced by the plaudits of their followers that the self-criticism which is the basis of constructive doubt is allowed to be carried away by the wind of complacency, and ceases to govern the way of life of the chosen person. At the same time, the disciples may have abdicated responsible control of their own lives and affairs, and placed themselves in the grasp of a possibly predatory leader who may subsequently abuse their trust for purely personal gain. This painful experience will have taught them something about their responsibility for their individual life and the power granted them as humans, but the lesson might be quite shattering. We have to learn that there is no worldly power that can be totally relied upon, 'Many waters cannot quench love, no flood can sweep it away; if someone were to offer for love all the wealth of his house, it would be laughed to scorn' (Song of Songs 8.7). This is not a cynical observation about human devotion so much as a realistic statement about human reliability in terms of self-giving love. The haste with which Peter withdrew from his betrayed Master shortly after swearing eternal allegiance to him (Matthew 26.35) is a telling example of the short-lived nature of our promises in the face of the world's challenge from day to day.

It was only with Christ's departure into death that the Holy Spirit could perform his amazing work of renewal on his disciples' lives (John 11.7). No matter how we interpret both the nature of God and his action in the world, we cannot deny his work in the lives of innumerable people. Here doubt can at least start to be appraised by facts.

But, of course, the question remains: were the Pentecostal phenomena true manifestations of a supernatural power or simply a type of group hysteria? This question makes me view the Divine Grace on a level far beyond psychical phenomena.

# 4 Doubt and personal relationships

To know another person entails something much more intimate than merely their outer appearance, their past history, or even their character as revealed by social contact. For all this is merely a surface effect which may be refreshing or depleting, depending on the sympathy or antipathy they invoke in us. None of us can claim the whole world as our friend because of the enormous range of character structure we show in our own lives. The fact that some people are alleged to be quite admirable in their dealings with others, need not necessarily shame us if we find them boring, sanctimonious or even religious bigots in their private lives, which spills over into their social contacts with others in the greater world around them.

This 'holier-than-thou' attitude not surprisingly irritates many less pious people who do not necessarily identify personal decency, a term with which they would feel more at home, with sanctity or holiness. When one considers the terrible intolerance of some Christian and other saints, in the appalling history of international religious persecution, one can sympathize with some of the misgivings which extreme religiosity evokes, especially in those who have suffered under this tyranny when they were very young.

Religion can still blight personal relationships, even though its authority and power are greatly diminished at present, as compared with even the fairly recent past. On the other side of the fence is the dogmatic atheist who is equally sure that their general attitude to the workings of creation is quite logically the only credible one, to the extent that all religion is dismissed to the category of primitive belief and superstition.

The one feature common to devout believer and atheist alike is their intransigent attitude to life. Being assured of their correctness in their belief, they are assured of the whole truth and cannot relate to any other type of person. Humans communicate primarily on a cerebral level, but if they cannot extend their capacities of relationships, they are sure to have a very limited understanding of their peers. As Shakespeare put it so memorably in *The Tempest*, IV, 1, 155, 'We are such stuff as dreams are made on and our little life is rounded with a sleep'. To many of us, perhaps schooled in orthodox psychotherapy, a dream is little more than 'the royal road to the unconscious', as Freud so memorably termed it, with the contents to be regarded as psychological more than deeply spiritual by many therapists. Enthusiasts of occult exploration would tend to give various interpretations of the essence of a dream.

We can relate also on a national level. In the not so distant past there was a shining aura of splendour around the countries of Western Europe with their magnificent tradition of art and science. Anyone educated in such an atmosphere carried with them an unconscious attitude of civilized urbanity, so that they could hardly help regarding other, non-Western nations with pity if not disdain. No doubt the state of their bank balance also played a part in establishing their self-esteem!

Only very recently has some measure of personal and social justice been accorded to various frequently degraded people, including the indigenous populations of most countries outside Europe. I personally am amazed that these people on the whole continue to behave so generously to their erstwhile white overlords, but we wait in trepidation to see for how long this state of magnanimity will persist, and how the economy will continue to thrive under a new management. Goodwill is central to national co-operation, but it should be underpinned by stern expertise if it is to effect something more than mere eloquence or feelings of affection.

When we encounter a person of high degree who comes from a distinguished background we tend to feel insecure, or even inferior, rather as the indigenous races of Africa or Australia may have felt. But, taking a leaf out of their book, we should concentrate our efforts on our own business, leaving others to follow their own devices. The work of an aboriginal community is concerned almost entirely with hunting and gathering food for the benefit of the community as a whole unit. Individual ownership is not a feature of their life.

We are wise to follow the final admonition of Candide, 'This is well said, but we must cultivate our garden'. This metaphor of Voltaire alludes to attending to our own affairs. The more we try to emulate others, the more frustrated and disillusioned we become, because we lose contact with our inner self. We also become more of a nuisance to others.

In addition to what has already been said, we also relate personally to a host of people whom we have known throughout our life. Knowing a person means being aware of their inner life, to the extent of being able to sympathize with their fears and aspirations and empathize with their feelings day by day. The difference between sympathy and empathy is that the former is a condition of shared emotion, mental state and feeling, whereas the latter is a power of projecting one's personality into and so comprehending the object of contemplation. The essence of empathy is full awareness of the present moment so that one's attention is riveted on the full expression of the person. This attitude of awareness would automatically go beyond the outer appearance or speech of the person but would instead see the state of soul which might belie our outer experience of satisfaction or happiness, to say nothing of faith and hope in a situation in which these qualities had little right to exist.

The more we are aware of another's state of mind, the more helpful we can be in assuaging their distress and pointing the way to faith and hope. To be sure, the fruits of the spirit, especially faith, hope, and love (1 Corinthians 13.13), come to us from another source which religious people would immediately identify with God. But we have to be open to receive these fruits, which we are then able to hand on at once to those around us, so that by collective effort the world may become a friendlier, less frightening place. As we are more ready to shed our fears and lose something of special value in itself, we instead discover that in giving ourselves unstintingly to our fellows, they come to know who they are more definitively. Therefore, when ceasing to cling to the transient, they come upon the long-lasting, and in this meeting something inside them is so changed from trivial impermanence to magnificent duration that a whole new world opens up into a place of breathtaking glory.

All real living is meeting, wrote Martin Buber in his spiritual classic *I and Thou*. When we meet someone else, whether known or unknown to us, something enclosed within us is unlocked and we flow out in peace, not only to that person but to the world in general. We forget about our limitations with their inevitable self-doubt as to whether we will be able to do what is required of us, and instead do the work unhesitatingly and with clear inner conviction. The encouragement of other people will become less necessary, except as a means of instruction in their particular disciplines, which will help us on our own chosen path, but we will be hindered much less by our own doubts and inhibitions.

In my own work of counselling and spiritual direction, I have learnt at first hand that when a client is desperate to find a way forward, and will apparently grasp any straw supplied, the important proceeding is under no condition to supply such a straw but to encourage the person to remain quiet and patient. If they really want to discover the way forward, it will be revealed to them at the right time. At present they are in all probability being groomed for things to come, and their immediate lesson is to learn how to remain calm and composed and to do such duties as come to them each day. These would relate primarily in caring for the state of their possessions, clothes, and general appearance. If these were in good condition a prospective employer would find them attractive members of their staff.

Personal relationships concern not only ourselves but also other people. There is not only the question of self-doubt but also of trusting the other party. This may involve a gamut of concern from a considerable financial or political group to a potentially intimate personal relationship where one reveals one's very heart to another individual. How can one ascertain the validity of such a relationship? The ultimate proof of such substantiality lies in the process of time – as the saying goes: 'The proof of the pudding is in the eating.' All this is obviously sound common sense, but is there any other way of knowing the correctness of a personal relationship at a much earlier stage?

I believe there are inner warnings audible to those who practise the deep silence which mystics would call contemplative prayer. Let it be said at once, I do not believe in a power outside ourselves who is open to our requests if we call upon him hard enough; twisting his elbow with sufficient vigour, to use an anthropomorphism. True prayer to me is silent openness to the universe, putting the continuous clamour of fear, desire, and negative feelings of anger, lust, and gluttony in our minds, completely to one side. Whatever power may govern the universe, conveniently called God, surely knows our needs and our distress sufficiently well enough not to require a description of them before action may be anticipated.

This is in my experience the natural healing power of life itself, associated with our own personalities, body, mind, soul, and spirit, which can be easily activated if we are still and open to the love which surrounds us, were we not receptive so seldom to its thrust. In this respect, I regard the soul as our inner self, the person who we truly are and assessed by our reactions to beauty, truth, and goodness or love. Admittedly, in this respect, beauty especially lies in the eyes of the beholder. While Pilate asked 'What is truth?' after Jesus had said to him 'For this I was born; for this I came into the world, and all who are not deaf to truth, listen to

my voice' (John 18.37–38). Goodness and love are also open
to grave misinterpretation, but nevertheless, the three taken
together can give us a good interpretation of the work of the
spirit, which is taken by religious people to be the means
within us whereby we are in contact with the source of these
three qualities above, and is an aspect of God.

The spirit within us would therefore be a part of the
universal Holy Spirit, by which we know, as far as we can
stretch in faith to this belief, the presence of God both in
ourselves and in the universe also. By this scheme, the spirit
would be the 'highest' part of the soul, just as the soul would
be the 'highest' part of the mind, which is the way of rational
thought in daily living. And when I write of height or depth
I am alluding to value in terms of superficiality or holiness,
for in principle these four qualities are all equally important
in the life of the human, from the body which generates life
from itself as well as magnificent art, to the spirit which is
the conveyor of inspiration from the supreme spirit of the
human soul and mind.

Every part of the person is in contact with the healing
power that surrounds it, as I have already affirmed. If you
remain in an attitude of openness silently, you will receive
healing on a very deep level. You simply have to be available.
There is no need and, indeed, a considerable blockage, if you
attempt to invoke the power by an act of will, somewhat like
magic. To a spiritual person, what I am referring to is grace,
the unmerited favour of God, but even to those who are
completely agnostic, the amazingly beneficial coincidences of
common life should make an impression of wonder upon
those who are completely aware of the joy of the present
moment.

The same train of thought can be applied to the relationships we have one with another. When we are working in a
harmony that comes from a reasonable trust, we are filled
with pleasure that leads us to relax our inner guard of
reticence and show our heart to other people. This attitude
carries with it both the doubt of the trustworthiness of those
with whom we are communicating and the careless abandon

of leaving our concerns with the knowledge of our acquaintances. We can attain this admirable state of self-abandonment to Divine Providence, to use a term that J. P. de Caussade uses so memorably in his spiritual classic of that name, if we have direct contact with God, which incidentally is considerably more than merely believing in God according to some theistic position. This inner knowledge comes from a soul that is open to the fullness of all relationships and is so radiant with joy that it does not need to hold on to any possessions belonging to itself, to the exclusion of anyone else.

At this stage of being, we can begin to understand some of Jesus' more extreme teachings. We start with the beatitudes: Matthew 5.3–12, and proceed to such exhortations as:

anyone who nurses anger against his brother must be brought to justice. Whoever calls his brother good for nothing deserves the sentence of the court. Whoever calls him fool deserves hellfire. So if you are presenting your gift at the altar and suddenly remember that your brother has a grievance against you, leave your gift where it is before the altar, first go and make your peace with your brother, and then come back and offer your gift. If someone sues you, come to terms with him promptly while you are on your way to the court, otherwise he may hand you over to the judge, and the judge to the officer and you will be thrown into jail. Truly I tell you, once you are there you will not be let out until you have paid the last penny. (Matthew 5.21–26)

Further teaching from Matthew 5 is contained in the final sentences,

You have heard that they were told, 'an eye for an eye, a tooth for a tooth'. But what I tell you is this: Do not resist those who wrong you. If anyone slaps you on the right cheek, turn and offer him the other also. If anyone wants to sue you and takes your shirt, let him have your cloak as well. If someone in authority presses you into service for one mile, go with him two. Give to anyone who asks; and do not turn your back on anyone who wants to borrow. You have heard that they were told 'Love your neighbour and hate your enemy'. But what if I tell you this: Love your enemies and pray for your persecutors. Only so can you be children of your heavenly Father who causes the sun to rise on the good and the bad alike, and sends the rain on the innocent and the wicked. There must be no limit to your goodness as your Heavenly Father's goodness knows no bounds. (Matthew 5.38–48)

This classical Christian teaching on detachment based on universal love must have been heard in innumerable churches over the last twenty centuries. But by the attitudes of the individual groups one to another, full of sectarianism, hatred, and mutual suspicion, it is obvious that inspiring words are far more easily grasped than generous deeds.

The question remains: are these teachings tractable to the broad masses? Doubt cannot simply be jettisoned, for truth is the nature of ultimate reality. The answer to this uncomfortable question is that we humans are morally weak and spiritually scarcely aware for most of our lives. There are exceptions to this depressing observation in the instances of the world's great religious geniuses, the saints of humanity, to which every denomination or religion may pay allegiance in their daily lives. But Jesus said the last word on the subject: the spirit is willing but the flesh is weak (Matthew 26.41).

The outer form of the belief system is as likely to provide one with the means of identifying oneself with the high and mighty of the land who subscribe nominally to the same system, as to guide one along the paths of true sanctity. And furthermore, one can so easily delude oneself about the nature of one's own piety; a fall from grace like that of innocent Job can bring one down to earth very quickly, and then we discover that there is no superficial agency that is immediately available to put everything right again, rather like a loving parent kissing the bruise of their child and soothing it with the reassurance of solicitude.

The question of the cause of human frailty which on a moral level can properly be equated with selfishness, an attribute hardly applicable to Job, is obscure. The nature of selfishness is sin, the tendency to place one's own interests in front of all other people's and to their detriment. The biblical allegory attributes human selfishness to a quality inherited from our primal ancestor Adam, who ate the fruit of the tree of knowledge of good and evil despite Divine interdiction, and was punished with his wife Eve accordingly (Genesis 3). This 'original sin' is much more probably a natural taint in the human personality, just as we are all subject to various bodily and mental diseases. If Adam and Eve were originally sinless, it seems unlikely that they would have fallen so easily into Satan's hands. It could, of course, be argued that inexperience lay at the root of their frailty, and here we are wise to leave the matter open to doubt.

In fact, only a fundamentalist would take the story of the fall literally. Its very great spiritual value lies, rather, in illuminating the necessity of obedience to the Divine Will. However we may interpret this aspect of creation, the same method of expounding spiritual truth is continually employed by Jesus in the Gospels where he frequently uses picturesque parables. The Old Testament example is seen in 2 Samuel 12.1–7. The parable is a fictitious narrative used to illustrate moral or spiritual relations, whereas an allegory is a narrative description of a subject under the guise of another subjectively similar subject. Thus, the stories of the Prodigal Son and the Good Samaritan are both wonderful parables, whereas the three stories of Matthew 25.10 (the Ten Wedding Attendants, the Talents, and the Last Judgement) are all fine allegories. Each in its own way gives the requirements necessary to enter the Kingdom of Heaven: alertness, using one's own gifts and talents properly and, above all, being constantly aware of the needs of others less fortunate than oneself.

This is the true nature of charity, in many respects a more suitable word than love, which is open to many misinterpretations. Love tends to be of variable quality, depending on the mood of the person, whereas charity may have a more constant character. This is another good example of the cleansing effect of doubt; that we take nothing for granted. Do not stifle inspiration, or despise prophetic utterances, but test them all; keep hold to what is good and avoid all forms of evil (1 Thessalonians 5.19–22).

This is as excellent an expression of doubt as we can find anywhere, but what exactly is good? Is it my particular point of view or frank prejudice, and is evil that which offends me personally? If these were correct definitions of these moral states, there would be no stability in our personal, national, or religious relationships, especially as we all tend to be very labile emotionally. The good is best considered as that which guides us towards emotional maturity in our personal relationships, whereas evil can be seen as a state of negativity, which emanates from ourselves and others also, that tends to undermine relationships and lead to general chaos. Above all, it causes us to turn against ourselves and others also, so that greater suffering may ensue. The good is constructive, whereas what is evil breaks down and destroys with malice and cruelty.

If we look at personal relationships in this context we can see the value of doubt, in a positive way. It leads us on to greater truth both about ourselves and others also. We can shed illusion and begin to live according to our true nature, needing to please nobody in order to placate them. If only we could function according to what we are as humans with our own individual stamp, we could give so much happiness to the world without even trying to do so!

The secret of a genuinely sincere relationship is a spontaneous outflowing to the other person, so that they and we are enriched and can do our respective duties better as a result of the meeting. Indeed, all real living is meeting, as we quoted Martin Buber earlier on in this chapter. But meeting is not dominating or speaking interminably. It is also intensive listening, even when all the parties are silent in prayer. This is true relationship in depth, just as they are all in contact with a deeper and also a higher source which religious people could justifiably call God.

# 5 Moods and assurance

We are all creatures of moods and these are liable to fluctuate alarmingly. The most exalted mood is one of generous self-giving. In this state of mind, one of feeling, we are able to transcend the barriers of self and enter the glorious state of the universe seen in terms, at least primarily, of our neighbour. Hence we are commended to love our neighbour as ourselves, our neighbour being, in the final analysis, all creatures no matter how noxious they may seem to us. They all spring from the common source and move to the common end. This is death and the unknown, the future that lies ahead of us all. When our state of mind, as a definition of a mood, is positive and outgoing, we feel that circumstances are all on our side, and our *joie de vivre* is ebullient. When, on the other hand, our mood is withdrawn, we are afflicted by a negative state of mind, a very unpleasant hollowness assails us, and we feel that we are useless for any of the world's demands, and suitable only for retirement and even, if necessary, death. It is not surprising that this negative state of depression may precipitate a suicide attempt if it is not confronted immediately and vigorously.

When we are taken over by a negative mood, doubt of a most destructive kind soon possesses our thinking processes. Why do I feel so rotten, what nastiness in my life lies at the root of this terrible depression? Is there an evil precipitating factor in myself, my environment, or in the source of all life? Whatever the answers to all these questions may be, I have no doubt that the final common path is the brain, which is controlled by chemical substances that influence its own workings and those of the other parts of the body also. I would unhesitatingly make the same statement about psychical experiences and mystical illumination also. Whatever their place of origin, the termination is the human brain where they can be rationally assessed with discrimination and acted on accordingly. In this way, we can communicate with one another in all the qualities of mind (the thinking processes), soul (the vale of moral and spiritual judgement in terms of beauty, truth and goodness or love), and spirit, where the ultimate creative process is known in mystical experience.

Paul speaks of this as 'Christ in you, the hope of glory' (Colossians 1.27). This is the experience of God that is recognized by theistic religion. The converse mood of ebullient joyfulness opens up on to the whole universe, seen as the ground of reality by those who have experienced it, and there is a great rejoicing from the relief of past tensions. Their minds are opened to fresh opportunities while their hearts beat in pleasant anticipation as new adventures open up to their entranced gaze. In such a positive frame of mind the whole person is infused with a power which is akin to the Holy Spirit of theistic religion. It is also called 'The Lord' and 'The Giver of Life'. In such a positive state of being, doubt fades away like the mist before a fresh summer day. This is as it should be, not because we are assured of such a condition of inevitable success in all our future endeavours, but because we are no longer attached by worldly concern to the exclusion of anything else. Inasmuch as now the worldly and the spiritual realms fuse and are transfigured into something of a new creation, therefore we can say that doubt is very much a part of our earthly consciousness, depending on our circumstances moment by moment.

When we once have moved from the temporal to the eternal, doubt evaporates. It does not simply disappear, for its potency actually increases like something resembling a homoeopathic remedy, and now it reinforces our own personality, strengthening it, and making it much more durable and positive. This example shows us that doubt which starts with a very considerable diffidence in the face of the 'authorities' who control world opinion can progress to the establishment of a completely new way of life. I am impressed with the words of Revelation 21.1–5:

> Then I saw a new heaven and a new earth, for the first heaven and the first earth had vanished, and there was no longer any sea. I saw the Holy City, new Jerusalem, coming down out of heaven from God, made ready like a bride adorned for her husband. I heard a loud voice proclaiming from the throne: 'Now God has his dwelling with mankind! He will dwell among them and they shall be his people, and God himself will be with them. He will wipe away every tear from their eyes. There shall be an end to death, and to mourning and crying and pain, for the old order has passed away!' The One who sat on the throne said, 'I am making all things new!'

In fact, doubt is as important for running our lives as it is for the workings of the universe. We in our childish attitudes long for a security, which, if granted, would imprison us in a world of mediocrity, governed by a hierarchy of unimaginative people who would automatically opt for stability and a dismal conformity at the cost of a spurious safety, whose end would be death rather than life. In this life one cannot have both safety and growth, because experience, on which development depends, is bound to traverse an uneven terrain, rather like a vehicle driven fast over rocky ground. Whether one survives the journey depends on the skill of the driver and the beneficence of the guiding power, who could be identified as the God of theistic religion.

When we travel at some speed over the uneven stretch of life, we need all the courage we can muster, no less than the faith that we can gather for the uneven ground ahead of us. The true antithesis of doubt is rather more than mere faith, which, to be frank, can have quite easily a certain static, dependent quality about it, if we relax into it too easily. The antithesis of doubt is even more than this easy faith; it is courage. This takes our own participation into the matter without fudging the issue, but gritting our teeth and carrying on, despite all evil omens. I am always reminded of a fine, but somewhat controversial hymn, which is strongly criticized by some Christians, but nevertheless has important things to say:

> Father hear the prayer we offer:
> Not for ease that prayer shall be,
> But for strength that we may ever
> Live our lives courageously.
>
> Not for ever in green pastures
> Do we ask our way to be;
> But the steep and rugged pathway
> May we tread, rejoicingly.
>
> Not for ever by still waters
> Would we idly rest and stay;
> But would smite the living fountains
> From the rocks along the way.
>
> Be our strength in hours of weakness,
> In our wanderings be our guide;
> Through endeavour, failure, danger,
> Father be Thou at our side.

The hymn is a direct criticism of the relaxing images of the peace summoned up in Psalm 23 with its green pastures and still waters. The final verse is to my mind especially pertinent.

> Be our strength in hours of weakness,
> In our wanderings be our guide;
> Through endeavour, failure, danger,
> Father be Thou at our side.

Life is not meant to be a permanent rest-cure where we can indulge our whims and pleasures indefinitely in the company of friends and servants. Once we have had the pleasure of such an enjoyable break from the routine of everyday existence, we have nothing to do but return once more to our work and help in the coming of the Kingdom, in whatever shape this Kingdom expresses itself in our minds, whether as a place of bodily healing, social justice, national *rapprochement*, or spiritual reconciliation, where the many, often hostile, religious groups, who strangely declare their worship of the same God, may come together in peace and reassurance. When we have understood the full nature of life, we understand with joy that service to the world around us is also universal service and its practice is perfect freedom. When we work in this frame of mind, in this mood, two apparently contrasting ways of experience come to our notice, tranquillity and action.

In the state of tranquillity we know the perfect peace of creation in God, depending on the system of belief of the individual, the peace with which the officiant blesses the congregation at the end of a church service, usually described as the peace of God which passes all understanding, that keeps their hearts and minds in the knowledge and love of God. This peace is the apogee of human awareness and carries us away from all personal care, bringing us to universal consciousness similar to that of the mystic. And yet the strange thing is that in this state of awareness we are closer to the sufferings of our fellow creatures than ever before. Yet we know with Julian of Norwich that 'all manner of thing shall be well'. In this process of spiritual transmutation we ourselves have been able to shed our customary self-concern and give ourselves body and soul to the sufferings of other people. This is the heart of tranquillity, the purest and most exalted way of growth through suffering and all that appertains to it.

Tranquillity is expressed in another famous hymn by John Greenleaf Whittier who was contemporary with Mrs Willis, the author of the hymn above:

Dear Lord and Father of Mankind,
Forgive our foolish ways.
Re-clothe us in our rightful mind,
In purer lives thy service find,
In deeper reverence praise.

In simple trust like theirs who heard,
Beside the Syrian sea,
The gracious calling of the Lord,
Let us, like them, without a word
Rise up and follow Thee.

O Sabbath rest by Galilee.
O calm of hills above,
Where Jesus knelt to share with thee
The silence of eternity,
Interpreted by love!

And now comes the climax of the hymn, where the tranquillity invoked by the vision of Jesus worshipping with the Father whom we call God, is drawn into our own souls also.

Drop thy still dews of quietness,
Till all our strivings cease;
Take from our souls the strain and stress,
And let our ordered lives confess
The beauty of thy peace.

Breathe through the heats of our desire
Thy coolness and thy balm;
Let sense be dumb, let flesh retire;
Speak through the earthquake, wind, and fire,
O still small voice of calm!

The mood expressed in this hymn is one of the utmost tranquillity, whereas Mrs Willis' hymn is pregnant with action, yet they come from a distinctly similar spiritual source: Whittier was a Quaker and Mrs Willis a Unitarian, both of the nineteenth century. Neither denomination subscribes to a formal creed and until the beginning of that century they, like the Jews, were denied various civil rights, at least in Britain. It is noteworthy that both denominations are miniscule when compared with the massive numbers of Catholics and fundamentalist Evangelicals, even in such an open society as that of Britain. Both Quakers and Unitarians fought for the religious emancipation of Catholics and Jews soon after their own acceptance on the religious scene, never having forgotten what rejection felt like. The Quakers have extended their witness to the complete rejection of all weapons of war, while the Unitarians have concentrated their activities largely in the direction of religious freedom. The Quakers fought against slavery right from the beginning of their ministry, whereas the Unitarians acted against this evil rather more slowly, though there were notable individual exceptions. The sad thing has been the decline in the influence of both denominations of what is loosely called 'liberal Christianity', which is in no small measure due to its rationalistic, 'scientific' bias.

It is interesting that the hymns I have quoted spring from a softer approach to reality unfettered by dogma. We live at present in an atmosphere of religious fundamentalism, whether Catholic or Evangelical; it is no wonder that many intelligent, well-educated people have turned their backs categorically on all religion, whereas not a few are experimenting with the religions of the East. I have no doubt that this essentially negative approach will wane and a new enthusiasm will materialize, but will it be a fashionable cult or individual figure from some exotic area of the world, or a real revelation that could lead a jaded humanity from illusion to an illumination about the nature of the creative process that could be called 'the spirit of God'? This is the real mood of assurance, because it will not depend on any promises from outside (they all turn out to be empty), but the inner transformation of the person themself. Only then can they be in control of the situation, and use the gifts (physical, mental, psychical, and spiritual) with which they have been endowed in a creative way to emulate the creative processes that typify the world itself. On the answer to this question hangs the future of humanity and the fate of the world, so closely linked are the human and the soil from which they spring in the universal creative process.

The way from constructive doubt to assurance is not from some dogmatic stance, but by the instruction of the spirit that governs the world. In this respect it is important to distinguish between dogma and dogmatism. Dogma is a principle, tenet, or doctrinal system, especially as laid down by the authority of the Church, whereas dogmatism is the arrogant declaration of an opinion, whether religious or secular. It often finds its most unpleasant expression in politics, finance or health-care. Dogma has to be expounded as a principle of teaching, and is conveyed to one person by another from their prior experience, or from what they themselves had previously been taught by their mentors.

We cannot communicate effectively by means of concepts, if we have not received the correct dogma, but once this has become dogmatic it is stifling and serves to quench the spirit in the most disastrous way. In the allegory of the good shepherd that occupies John 10 there is a memorable analogy: 'I have come that they may have life, and may have it in all its fullness' (John 10.10). This life is the power that moves and controls the world and infuses all its inhabitants with the joy of being alive and adding their contribution. Through this vital power, the strangling nature of dogmatism, that converts necessary dogma into a cemetery of dead concepts that had their day perhaps centuries ago, is changed into a fresh source of truth, which was always present but until then completely occluded by obsolete concepts. These were the residue of old, ignorant prejudices, whose presence prevented the way forward of progressive dogma, whether this took the form of scientific research, religion, or psychical studies.

The last never fails to evoke the derision of 'scientific' people or the revulsion of the 'religious enthusiast', but it is nevertheless a *bona fide* means of communication, both between two living people and between the living and the dead. I personally have had sufficient unsought experience to know the evidential truth of what I write here. I have little doubt, however, that if a person strains desperately for a living proof in one who has made the great transition that we call death, they will never be fully satisfied, especially if they are unwise enough to consult a 'medium'. This is primarily because the various entities that invade the consciousness of the medium (or sensitive) have no authority, and are very likely to be fraudulent. This is no special reflection on the medium but on the dubious material with which they are working.

If anyone wants desperately to get a message from the 'dear departed', there is a good chance of their heart's desire being fulfilled. The essential question remains: who or what is fulfilling the earnest desire? It is here that the most critical doubt is mandatory. The annals of psychical research are full of fraud, illusion, and disgusting dishonesty on the part of the research worker. The other side of the picture is much more kindly, but it needs all the honesty of the detached worker to disentangle the mess and find an answer approximating the truth.

If there is any field where the sharpest doubt is absolutely essential, it is parapsychology, previously known as psychical research. Many bereaved people have been the helpless victims of charlatans who trade on their loneliness and sorrow. Most of the material that is brought through is largely guesswork based on the knowledge cleverly evoked from the client by the medium, but sometimes there may be an additional element of telepathy from client to medium.

All this can be quite impressive to the person who is ignorant about the tricks that the mind can play. The whole field of parapsychology is best left to the investigation of a specialist in this area. The biblical prohibitions against communication with the dead are best fully regarded for their sake as well as ours (Leviticus 19.31; 20.6, 27; Deuteronomy 18.11). I would add a caveat to this stern prohibition against communicating with the dead: if they communicate with us quite spontaneously and unsought, we are entitled to listen to their message.

I personally have been given information quite spontaneously by my father and various friends which turned out to be surprisingly accurate. To me there is a constant interplay of information between the living and the dead. This may be a vehicle for the transference of knowledge in our world, especially in the fields of art, science, and social concern. It may be a way of cleansing discernment also, the apogee of honest, constructive doubt. How do we know for certain that the unexpected message is true? For this degree of veracity to be attained, we need absolute confirmation of our doubts. And that has proved virtually impossible in the discipline of parapsychology so far. I personally do not believe that we are at the present time fitted for psychic communication, either with our living peers or with those who are now dead to the flesh. Such psychic communication as occurs at present, as I have already indicated, I believe to be of a debased type, subject to fraud by the 'medium' and by those 'on the other side', as the living dead are so frequently described by spiritualists. They earn their living by transmitting messages from the dead to those who are still alive, or to be more precise, it is their mediums who do the transmission and earn the money.

But I do believe that a time will come, and perhaps in a future nearer than we can envisage at present, when we will be able to communicate with one another, both in the here and now and after we have 'shuffled off this mortal coil', as Shakespeare puts it in *Hamlet*, III, 1, 50. This will be accurate psychic communication transmitted spiritually. Its content will be truly spiritual and no longer merely spiritualistic. The Holy Spirit will infuse it and the real God, no longer a figment of doubt, will govern it. But until this visionary future event materializes, the most critical doubt is crucially important. Like a keenly sharpened knife adequate to split a very molecule in half, so this doubt must be able to cut away all accretions that have attached themselves to human conduct and character from the very beginning of the race.

Doubt is the cleansing mechanism of the mind. It removes all attitudes of embarrassment, of feeling one ought to be charitable to a concept when one knows perfectly well it is nonsensical, of giving a person the benefit of discretion, when one knows they are unworthy of it and are liable to be a great nuisance to those around them, by trying a remedy when one knows perfectly well that it will not help one, no matter how efficacious it may be for someone else.

As we saw in Chapter 1, self-doubt can be crippling and is not to be recommended. But self-criticism is doubt of a different stamp and can always, within reason, be commended, since it holds us open to the constructive criticism of our neighbours and the world generally. Doubt as we have already seen, is the challenge of courage. And it also stimulates it into action.

# 6 The enigma of God

Does God really exist or is this a figment of the human imagination? Can we do without God? Is the idea of God a proof of human weakness, so that unless we have him close to us we cannot really have any trust in our own strength? Does he, as it were, fill the petrol tank with petrol in our car, so that we can then move on? Without him, on the other hand, the car would remain stationary. All these are vital questions. The concept of God has never been easy to accommodate. The second chapter, which dealt with Job and his terrible experience with God and the suffering associated with it, makes this a vital question which none of us can possibly avoid.

The first thing about God, if we believe in God at all, is that God is a living god; not involved merely in the creation, but also in its growth and its development. One can say this dogmatically, because unless God is a living god we cannot know him, and in a strange way, we cannot know ourselves either. A god who is real is one who is real to us and makes us into something whom we know to be real. I know my name and my being because an essence of the life of the spirit, the Holy Spirit whom I have mentioned on a number of occasions so far, infuses my being, and makes me realize that I am significant in my own right, not because I am especially important, but because I live and I can contribute to life and to the life of other people.

This, incidentally, is ultimately the purpose of my own life, a life which has been recently very much hindered by serious locomotor problems with severe pain. Over the last year I have hardly been able to walk at all, and I can see my purpose as a human being only in the way that I can help other people by writing and speaking to them in a way that can alleviate their own suffering; so, although I am a cripple, I am nevertheless useful to other people by what I can do for them. In a way this is God the Holy Spirit working through me and proving to me, even as he proved to Job, that there is a use in my life, even though it is in a mess and has nothing to offer at this particular moment. I am not ashamed to be emotional at this time, because it is only in showing ourselves as we truly are that we may give ourselves to other people. The unemotional individual who will not share their own suffering, their own pain, their own death and resurrection, is not only useless to the world but actually does not exist as a real person.

It is on this level that we may begin to understand the nature of God. God is a living god, and a god who lives is one who suffers with his creation and will not ultimately leave them until he has re-created them. To me this is what Jesus is about. He died in order that we might live, and in his new life a new creation is born, which may replace all that is sordid by something of the full nature of a full human being.

If we cannot see God in this light, I do not think that we are seeing the real God. This other god becomes a sort of artefact, something artificial that we can put in his place, something that we can use according to our own intellectual fascination, but who has no substantial reality at all. That is why God is a living god and not only an instrument of our satisfaction. If God exists, he exists in order that I may grow into something of his measure, which is the same as into the measure of the form of Jesus Christ himself.

One should always try to see oneself clearly, neither being unnecessarily sentimental nor, on the other hand, denigrating oneself. To be a human is a very great privilege. We can think, feel, act, and do much good. The great works of art in human history are a splendid tribute to the creative function of the human being, especially in the lives of the great spiritual geniuses. Furthermore, in the Word who became flesh and dwelt among us, we can see what it could be to be a real human being.

Why did God create us? He created us out of love. Love is the basis of creation, just as love is the basis of the creation of a child when a man and woman come together. They do not plan to have a child, not directly at any rate, they come together out of love and in the act of making love a child is born. They do not think about the child so much as their concern one for another. But the outcome of that love is the creation of a new individual. That is why sexual intercourse is one of the holiest actions that a human can perform, although it is enjoyed with so much frivolity and irresponsibility in everyday life. But until we can see the glory of the human being as a person who creates, we cannot understand the nature of humanity and the human as a way to the perfection of God. This gives us an understanding of what God is trying to do to us and for us. And until we know God properly, we cannot know his purpose, or our purpose either.

God is not a being that has been thought of, or created out of our own mind. God is the basis of our life, and through him our minds develop and grow into a new understanding of reality. This is the difference between the Christian, or at any rate the spiritual understanding of life, and the purely mechanistic or atheistic one. The atheist sees life as something that is to be created for the purpose of the human being on a purely utilitarian level, and is not afraid or ashamed to kill or destroy anything that does not help them, or gets in their way, whereas when we move towards the spiritual way of life, we give of our lives absolutely to the world and through the world to our common humanity. When we grow in the love of humanity, when we become full human beings, we begin to realize that Jesus is not merely the prototype of God, but that we are all born in the form of Jesus and in that humanity of Christ at large.

The end of our life is to become Christs, so that the world may become a world that is Christian in the sense that all human beings have a Christian identity, and through human

59

beings all other forms of life also. But they could never attain to our stature because of our own superior spiritual, psychical, and mental development. Nevertheless, those who understand domesticated animals can see that even this statement could be arrogant and ill-informed.

Jesus came into the world in order that we might enter into the full life of God and actualize the abilities which lie latent within us, and until we can do this we will never be fully human. In other words, the knowledge of God involves the knowledge of ourselves in the form of Christ. Many people will say this is idealistic nonsense. How many people have attained this knowledge, when one thinks of the horrors that our own century have brought on us: the terrible dictatorships, the cruelties, the explosions of one type or another, the mass killings of innocent people. But the fact that we can react so violently against this proves that we have an inner depth of knowledge as well, which will never be satisfied by a merely experiential understanding of reality!

It is evident that the way of life is the way of meaning. If there is no meaning, our lives soon disintegrate. The meaning of our life is one of concern for others, primarily human beings, but then for animals, plants, and everything that grows. It shows itself in our attitude to each other and also in our response to the great arts of the world, especially music, literature, and the pictorial arts. In all of these we grow from mere animals to people of great sensitivity. We cannot escape long without a deep awareness of the nature of relationships coming to us, and it is here that we may begin to sense the meaning of God. This God is not a god who is a pleasant god. We saw this in the story of Job, in the second chapter of this book, in the great study of the Wisdom Literature of the Old Testament, and we know it in our own lives only too well. What sort of god can it be that has allowed countless holocausts to occur, droughts, earthquakes, many natural disasters, the cruelty of human beings to which has been added the suffering coincident on natural disasters of one type or another? And yet we have been given a mind, a mind resident in the brain, we might say, and this will never be satisfied until it grasps an answer.

To be a human being is a very great privilege. The fact that we suffer so much does not detract from the privilege at all; it makes the privilege all the more poignant. This chapter started in a mood of tears and now it moves towards a mood of triumphant assurance. I am now at peace in myself and at peace with the world; I am no longer sad, either at the world or at my own state of infirmity. All these seem somehow to have evaporated before the great mystery of relationships and healing. I myself now feel healed; not in terms of bodily function but in terms of my mind. I no longer am filled with self-pity of any type, nor do I care what happens to me on a purely physical level. I know that whatever I do will be done according to the assurance of God, and that all the gifts that I have will be used according to what I can give to other people; whether I can move about or not is irrelevant.

What alone is relevant is what I can give while I am still alive. To be alive is the greatest of all privileges. While we are here we can do so much and help so many people. Some help by activity, others help merely by being quiet and listening. Some help by giving of themselves in terms of artistic creativity of one type or another. It is only when we start to compare ourselves with others and feel that we are not getting our just due as compared with them that we really do go off course and cause both ourselves and others a great deal of trouble. This is the one thing that I have thoroughly learnt by bitter experience. I knew it always, of course, intuitively, but now I know it in terms of direct experience as well. It does not matter at all whether I will ever be able to walk properly or not; what does matter is that I can give assurance to other people, and write the types of books that I have been writing, especially recently, because in them there is a spark of truth and hope that can joyfully be given to others and help them on their way.

This is not a sort of reassurance or trying to make the best of a bad situation but is seeing life as it is in the raw, and giving of oneself as perfectly as one can to other people.

Only in this way can one begin to do the work that was set out for one. In any life there is tragedy. Some people like Job suffer rather late in life; others, like young children who get cancer, have a terrible death early in life. But it really does not matter at all. What does matter is how they die. Job was alive and relatively well cared for with plenty of the good things of life before tragedy struck him; many young people have died of cancer in their earlier years when they were still adolescent, but what matters is that they may understand and see something of the nature of reality. It is well known that young children who die of cancer, particularly tumours of the brain, seem to have a wisdom that their parents do not possess at all. Far from needing to be consoled by their parents, they try to console them, so that when they do die, their parents will be in a better position to bear their particular bereavement. This degree of maturity is absolutely marvellous; it tells us also how very impermanent our lives are and how wrong we are in so much of what we believe is real and what is unreal. We do not know the difference between reality and unreality because we feel that everything ought to suit our requirements, and that it is wrong when we fail to get our own way.

When we are still we can begin to see the nature of reality, and then we can begin to know who God really is; not an anthropomorphic image. The type of god who appears in the Old Testament is certainly not the real God, he is what would be called 'Nobodaddy', particularly by William Blake.

William Blake, one of the great prophetic geniuses of our culture, swore that the god of Reason was not the same as the god of Imagination. He called that rationalistic god 'Nobodaddy', the title added later in a different coloured ink!

The difference between the real God and the god of jealousy or 'old Nobodaddy' is that the latter is a human construct, the human mind working on its own deistic and ultimately atheistic principle and finding a being of its own with which it works and makes contact. It is not still and does not know the one true God, which is the god of reality.

Atheism is a frank disbelief in the existence of God, whereas deism is a frank construct of a god without accepting prior revelation. It is a type of 'natural religion', and is useful for the active human mind in trying to explain the phenomena of the universe. But it has no autonomy, nor any caring for its creatures. Deism is a type of worship of the human mind, which has formed a creature that can act according to what humans desire. In both deism and atheism the object of worship is the human; as we all know, the result is the emergence of a god of selfish, amoral power.

It is only when we can know that we ourselves know nothing at all, and can learn to be still and listen, that the one true God can come to us and inspire us, and form us in his own image; otherwise, we try to inspire God and tell him what to do and form him in our own image. The result is destructive and evil, and this has been the god that man has fashioned and worshipped in modern times, and it has also been the god of much 'religion', if one is honest about it. Priests and people alike have worshipped this idol, whom they have made in their own image and elevated in the form of various religious leaders. Now, as a religious leader, but in their own form, they can decide what should be done in human terms.

Why art thou silent and invisible,
Father of Jealousy?
Why dost thou hide thyself in clouds
from every searching Eye?
Why darkness and obscurity
in all thy words and laws,
That none dare eat the fruit but from
the wily serpent's jaws?
Or is it because Secrecy gains females' loud applause?

This was Blake's poem against *Nobodaddy*, which really means nobody's daddy of course, the hypothetical father of all, which was Blake's jocular nickname for Urizen, the father of jealousy.

Here is more of Blake's meditation:

Are not the joys of morning sweeter than the joys of night?
Are not the vig'rous joys of youth ashamèd of the light?
Let age and sickness silent rob the vineyards in the night;
But those who burn with vig'rous youth
pluck fruits before the light.
They said this mystery never shall cease;
The priest promotes war,
And the soldier peace.

Love to faults is always blind;
Always is to joy inclin'd;
Lawless wing'd and unconfin'd;
And breaks all chains from every mind.

Deceit to secrecy confin'd;
Lawful, cautious and refin'd:
To anything but interest blind,
And forges fetters for the mind.

That, of course, is the whole point about the mystery of God.
When we are quiet we can know something of what we
believe about God, and 'wisdom' comes flowing into our
being, and then we can understand that when we search and
find, we tend to form an image in our own mind, in other
words, a pure heresy, making God in our own image; and
that image is a travesty of the human being. Whatever it says
is plausible but basically wrong, and in its place we might
have something that is quite evil.

The same applies to religion. Most of the leaders of
religion, the various prelates of one type or another, are
equally unsatisfactory, if not evil. But they have been given
the place of honour in churches and other places of religious
worship. If we were quiet, we would know the true word of
God, and that word would guide us to the right church and
the right leaders.

Why do we behave in this foolish way? Not only are we
unsure of our own judgements, but there is a desire in all of
us that we may be proved right and the others wrong. This
applies particularly in the realm of religion, of course, where
nobody knows the right answer. There is absolutely no
certainty in any religion, but when we are quiet Christ comes

to us in the form that we know, in terms of our being, and then we start to do the right work.

We will never know Christ by reading a book about him, or thinking about him, but if we are still he comes to us, and we see him in a new form and then the light of reality dawns on us as well, and we at last do the right thing and work in the right way. If I were to tell you what was right and what was wrong, I would simply be giving you my own opinions, and they would be bound to be wrong, if for no other reason than I would be trying to impress you with my own spirituality. But if I admit that I do not know, and am still and quiet, we can work together and be inspired, and then we will know the right way.

True knowledge, in other words, is not so much experimental as experiential; when we know that we know nothing, we can know the power of God within us, and start to do the right thing. Then there is nothing interfering with our own senses and understanding. But when we come knowing the right answer, we ourselves get in the way and the results are always bad, sometimes very bad indeed.

When we think of the evil that has been done in the name of religion, particularly theistic religion – the religion of the West, in other words – we can see that the god of theistic religion has been a very intrusive entity who has been built up on the desires and understandings of human beings. We have worshipped him rather than known him. We have worshipped a form made up in our own mind rather than being quiet and listening.

'Thou shalt love the Lord thy God with all thy heart, and with all thy soul, and with all thy mind, and with all thy strength' (Mark 12.30). But this god is often only a human artefact full of the human problems of fear and the desire for power. There is ignorance and general prejudice associated with the god that most people, particularly of the West, worship. This is ridiculous in the East where there is quieter, much more still, worship, and here God may be known in quietness and worshipped in unostentatious devotion.

You will never come to the fullness of reality by thought.

'By love may he be gotten and holden but by thought never.' These are the words that we remember so well from that great mystical treatise, *The Cloud of Unknowing.* We can never know God by our mind alone. We tend to make God into an idol so easily, and that idol soon becomes our dictator as well. The God that we make is the god that we want. And he is a god that does what we want him to do for us. We, on the other hand, do not usually listen to the great voice of eternity that leads us on to ultimate reality. Only when we have gone beyond the quietness and stillness of our own being to the reality of the eternal can we know what God really wants of us and what his nature is.

The enigma of God is that he never makes any demands on us at all. He merely shows us the way, but we are to follow according to our own will. If we do not want to follow on, we can get stuck and killed, and we will never produce anything worthwhile. But if we are humble, we will learn something about which even the greatest intellects of the age were completely ignorant, and then we, and ultimately they as well through our example, will begin to understand.

The point about God is that nothing positive can be said about him until we know that nothing negative cannot be said about him. When we know that nobody can know God, then, in a strangely paradoxical way, he shows himself to us and we begin to live the life that Christ lived, and we see that in Christ, God shows himself to us at all times, in all places, and throughout all lives.

Praise be to God.

# 7 The benefit of an attitude of doubt in life

What shall I bring when I approach the Lord? How shall I stoop before God on high? Am I to approach him with whole offerings or yearling calves? Will the Lord accept thousands of lambs or ten thousand rivers of oil? Shall I offer my eldest son for my own wrongdoing, my children for my own sin? God has told you what is good and what it is that the Lord asks of you: only to act justly, to love loyalty, and to walk wisely before your God.

This passage from Micah 6.6–8 is a classical description of what God requires of us to live the life that leads to fullness of being.

This chapter describes the way by which we may come to the knowledge of God. We come to God primarily by being silent. This I described in my last chapter, where we understood that we cannot know God by the intellect at all, and that the best we can do about God is to be quiet before him. By love he may be gotten and holden, but by thought never.

It is our capacity to worship the mind in its thinking aspect that has caused us so much trouble in our modern life, and produced so few fruits in return. Thought is essential, indeed, we could not exist without it, and our modern advances in science, technology and other important aspects of current life could not occur without it. But the question remains, what are we aiming at when we do these things? It is a wonderful thing to be able to cure disease by modern technology, but what have we put in its place? Is one disease to succeed another, or are we to follow in a new direction and lead a healthy life? Are we to enjoy life, simply to follow one problem after another in a bovine way by satisfying the intellect? The problem with stilling our lives is that we have deified the mind in its intellectual capacity. To know more and more is the object of many people's lives; more and more about less and less would be a very good way of describing our present situation. It is not merely less and less knowledge in terms of quantity; it is also less and less in terms of quality. We know so little about what is really important in life that, in the end, we are speechless before the immensity of absolute ignorance. God is never known by the intellect trying to thrust itself forward and dominate the world. If it does this successfully, it would simply destroy the world. Such things as nuclear explosions in our own time have emphasized this only too eloquently, and these are only the beginnings of things that could be equally or even more intensively destructive. It is when we know how to be quiet before God, and still in love, that we may begin to undergo an unfolding of consciousness and see what is unseen or, preferably, invisible, to many highly intellectual people.

What is that which is often visible to the poorly educated person and completely invisible to the ultra-educated intellectual? It is the glory of life itself. What has life to offer; what has God given us in this brief spell we have on this earth? It is concentrated on the five senses, not merely in terms of registering various things, but through that registration coming to understand the glory of being alive at all. To be able to hear, for instance, is not only wonderful in its own right, but we can hear other people speak, and converse with them, and be inspired by the most marvellous music in the world. This music itself may convey little to most people, but its emotional impact can change a person's whole life. In the same way, sight merely makes us aware of various objects in our vicinity, but if we see clearly, we see the reality behind the object, whether it is material, physical, or artistic. Take a painting as another instance: there is little substance in it apart from the paint itself, but the thought and feeling behind it can change a person's entire perspective on life. The same applies to touch, smell, and taste.

When we are aware of God, we can sense the underlying reality that is at the basis of all the things that we can comprehend with our five senses: sight, taste, touch, smell, and hearing are worthless if there is nothing behind them that can be the basis of their recognition, but once we can recognize them, they cease to become merely something we can use, but are now something that can inform us about reality.

Reality is not with us for very long; our days of life are very short. I quoted this in our very first chapter. Our days are short and full of misery; but if we know what we are seeing there is no more misery, and life becomes one of joy and pleasure. If, on the other hand, we cannot see the reality behind the form, we are ignorant and our lives are death even before they are really over. Job thinks of himself as dead, even before he has come to the peak of his existence of misery. When things went wrong with him he was tempted to give up life completely. He wished only for death. 'The thing I feared most in life has come upon me', he said (Job 3.25). If he had been wiser, he would have realized this was the great test of his life, the great experience of reality.

Reality does not consist primarily of having a good time or enjoying all the benefits of the world; it comes of knowing what God is and what we are to be in the fullness of our creation. We are much more than flesh and blood; we are thoughts and, through thoughts, actions that can change the whole world. Man does not live on bread alone but on every word that comes from the mouth of God, as Jesus told the devil, in the second of his three temptations in the wilderness (Matthew 4.4).

The human being does not understand these things at all; they are hidden from him, until the time of his death. To many of us death is the ultimate failure of life, and to keep alive as long as possible is the most important thing we can do. This is a tragedy; not because we should strive to keep alive as long as possible, but because our lives often have so little meaning because of our ignorance.

The purpose of life is, first of all, relationships with other people, second, enjoying the gifts of the senses that God has given us, and third, and perhaps most important of all, to be able to actualize our own talents, so as to give as much as possible to the world around us. When we can actually give of ourself to others, our lives are entering into the fullness of being, and then we can appreciate the sort of statement that Micah makes in relationship to what God desires of us.

> What shall I bring when I approach the Lord? How shall I stoop before God on High? Am I to approach him with whole offerings or yearling calves? Will the Lord accept thousands of lambs or ten thousand rivers of oil? Shall I offer my eldest son for my own wrongdoing, my children for my own sin? God has told you what is good and what it is that the Lord asks of you: only to act justly, to love loyalty and to walk wisely before your God.

These are the things that God has called us to do. To act justly is to see your fellow human being, and indeed your fellow creature, as a being in their own right, and to love and to do everything possible to justify their lives and to make them more tolerable, so that everyone may get what is their due and no one may be swindled out of any of it. To love loyalty means to love all that is good and to live a life of loyalty to others, no longer behaving in a way that is deleterious or in any way wrong; but, on the other hand, to love all that brings people to the closeness of God. And finally to walk wisely before your God; that means to watch your step, to thank God for the gifts that you have in terms of material progress. I spoke in a previous chapter about my own painful infirmity at present, because my legs are not working properly. If you walk wisely before the Lord, you will never be in a state like this; not that I attribute my particular condition to anything wrong that I did, but it is a particular lesson that I, like Job, have had to learn in order to become a wiser, more considerate individual.

We will later think again about Job, what his sufferings meant, and why he had to undergo them. I went through this stage of a Job experience on a superficial level before, although the meaning probably was quite deep enough. In

the end, it is the very heart of suffering. Why do we all have
to have pain of one type or another? The worst pain of all is
probably that of parents who see their little children die of
cancer or in accidents. This seems so completely pointless,
cruel, and unloving. Who has gained by such a thing?
Certainly not the children; probably the parents to a certain
extent in that they have to learn that nobody has any
proprietorship over their particular family, but in the end it
is a terrible experience for all involved. Yet who knows what
is involved in such an experience as this. And what about
those who have been involved in killing others in accidents
and similar sorts of tragedies? Where would you rather
stand: as the victim of an accident, or the cause of an
accident that kills somebody else? A terrible question to
answer! I know what the right answer should be, but I too
shudder to think of myself being maimed or killed through
somebody else's negligence or folly. And yet this goes on day
after day. It is part of our life on earth, and nobody can
escape the implications of everyday life for one second.

It is important also to face these facts squarely without
trying in any way to avoid them, because this is how we
grow. Some people will say that if that is what growth
entails, they would rather not have it at all. But in a more
sober frame of mind your assessment would be a more sober
one as well, and you would see that growth and life are
absolutely concurrent. If you stop growing you die, and
nobody wants to die. If you have to die, die rather as a result
of a dreaded disease or an accident than of legal punishment
or of pure inanimacy. These are terrible thoughts, but ones
that have to be faced in clear consciousness.

A great book in the Wisdom Literature of the Old Testament is Ecclesiastes. It certainly disillusions one of many
attitudes of false hope, and yet it is by no means lacking in
humour. Towards the end of chapter 6 we find the dictum:

> The end of all man's toil is but to fill his belly, but his appetite is
> never satisfied. What advantage then in facing life has the wise
> man over the fool, or the poor man for all his experience? It is
> better to be satisfied with what is before your eyes than give

reign to desire; this too is emptiness and chasing the wind. Whatever has already existed has been given a name, its nature is known; a man cannot contend with that which is stronger than he. The more words one uses, the greater is the emptiness of it all; and where is the advantage to a man? For who can know what is good for a man in this life, this brief span of empty existence through which we pass like a shadow? Who can tell a man what will happen next here under the sun?

A good name smells sweeter than the finest ointment, and the day of death is better than the day of birth. Better to visit the house of mourning than the house of feasting. For to be mourned is the lot of every man, and the living should take this to heart. Grief is better than laughter: a sad face may go with a cheerful heart. Wise men's thoughts are at home in the house of mourning, but a fool's thoughts are in the house of mirth. The laughter of a fool is like the crackling of thorns under a pot. This too is emptiness. Slander drives a wise man crazy and breaks a strong man's spirit. Do not be quick to show resentment; for resentment is nursed by fools. Do not ask why the old days were better than these; for that is a foolish question. Wisdom is better than possessions and an advantage to all who see the sun. Better have wisdom behind you than money; wisdom profits men by giving life to those who know her.

Consider God's handiwork; who can straighten what he has made crooked? When things go well be glad, but when things go ill consider this: God has set the one alongside the other in such a way that nobody can find out what is to happen next. In my empty existence I have seen it all, from a righteous man perishing in his righteousness to a wicked man growing old in his wickedness. Do not be over-righteous and do not be over-wise. Why make yourself a laughing-stock, do not be over-wicked and do not be a fool. Why should you die before your time? It is good to hold on to the one thing and not lose hold of the other; for a man who fears God will succeed both ways. Wisdom makes the possessor of wisdom stronger than ten rulers in a city. The world contains no man so righteous that he can do right always and never do wrong. Moreover, do not pay attention to everything men say, or you may hear your servants disparage you. For you know very well how many times you yourself have disparaged others.

Whatever has happened lies beyond our grasp, deep down, deeper than man can fathom. I went on to reflect. I set my mind to enquire and search for wisdom and for the reasoning of things, only to discover that it is folly to be wise and madness to act like a fool. The wiles of a woman I find mightier than death. Her heart is a trap to catch you and her arms are fetters. The man who is pleasing to God may escape her. But she will catch a sinner. So says the speaker, this is what I have found. Reasoning things out one by one; after searching long without success, I have found one man in a thousand worth the name, but I have not found one woman among them all. This alone I have found: that God when he made man, made him straight-forward, but man invents endless subtleties of his own. (Ecclesiastes 7.25–29, especially verse 29)

This particular dictum about human nature is very telling. We tend to complicate things. The trouble with women, if one takes this particular passage seriously, and personally I reject sexism of any type, is that they are more emotionally active and powerful than men and they know what they want. What they want is often ultimately trivial. They want to possess. Men want to possess things; women want to possess men and human beings generally. Both attitudes are destructive. You cannot possess without destroying.

If I want to possess you for instance, I could squeeze you, in the same way as a boa constrictor. I have had this practised on me, and I know how it feels, and yet the woman who did it would not even have understood why she was so repulsive to me. It is really an attitude of insecurity; the same insecurity that a man has when he wants to make as much money as he can or attain as high a position as he can in society. All this is sheer futility. Supposing I were to attain great riches or a grand social position, where would it get me in the end? Merely ageing, retirement, disease, futility, and death. That is the common end of all human beings. The Buddha actually made this more simple: what is in store for all of us is ageing, disease and death, he would have said, and this is perfectly true.

There is nothing wrong with this; it is the way of all flesh and, if it were not so, the world would soon be so over-crowded that nobody would be able to survive at all. But none of us wants to grow old; we certainly do not want to greet old age, with its diminishing powers of body and mind, and death is completely intolerable, except to those wise people who see it as the ultimate friend of all life. But if we can reach that degree of wisdom, then we can be friends with all people, because we are no longer in conflict with them or trying to beat them at their own game.

As one grows older, so one should be prepared to dispense more and more with one's reputation. One should begin to help those who are younger than oneself, and give it away to them, so that what was once ours in terms of reputation, wealth, and power, now goes to them, and we can become their parents, fathers or mothers, as the case may be.

It is much more important to act as a beneficent parent to a younger person than to try and beat them at their own game. Then at least one has no enemies, and has a greater intimation of what friendship is really about. The more I can support and help you, the more I can be a friend of yours. The more I become an adversary of yours, the more I enter into competition with you, and the more you fear and hate me. The end is pure pity for a decrepit old person whose pride would be hurt by the need for urgent outside help.

It is interesting to read the critiques of books written by older people who were quite well known in their youth. These critiques show an unpleasant attitude towards those who now are quite obviously on a higher level of understanding, at least in the world as it now is. Jealousy colours their criticism, and what they say clearly is full of dislike, even contempt and hatred. Obviously they feel that they have never really fulfilled their promise adequately, and others have profited from their particular inspiration, and now they are intent on getting their own due back. This is very unfortunate indeed, and it shows how sad it is when people cannot face their true selves adequately.

When we can live our lives as they should be lived and

enjoy the fruits of our labours and also the gifts that God has given us, we can start to be fulfilled individuals, no longer trying to impress other people or prove that we are better than they are. This is the way forward in any life on earth. At last we are fully ourselves and now do not need to prove that we are better than anyone else. Life on this level is one of impressive joy. Now we can actually help those who are younger and less experienced than we are, and bring them to the joy of actualizing their own gifts and personalities, so that they too can convey their own personal insights into the larger personal arena.

If I have to prove that I am the best of them all, I almost invariably am inferior. But if I can forget myself entirely and give of myself to the great thrust of life, then I can give something that is absolutely irreplaceable. We all have so much in ourselves that is irreplaceable because we are all individuals and made in the shape and form of God, according to what he has made us; at the same time, there are in us all the Spirit of God and also our individual spirit, which makes us unique individuals. If we deny our uniqueness or try to prevent others showing their own personality, we become inadequate people and the Spirit of God does not function properly within us: instead, we become more and more dependent on attitudes which we should have left behind years ago.

It is worthwhile recalling the dictum I have recently cited: 'This alone have I found: that God, when he made man, made him straightforward, but man invents endless subtleties of his own' (Ecclesiastes 7.29). Why do people behave in this way? Why do they create difficulties out of sheer ignorance? Is it because their own perverse character has made them want to do things in a more complicated and also a more dishonest way? They want to draw out of life much which is completely fallacious and in so doing they have produced endless misery for themselves and for others as well. The more one tries to prove that one is better than others, that one's way is by far the best, the more one in the end fails in one's intentions.

Only when we forget ourselves and do the work that God has given us to do with joy and abandon and the submission of joy and peace in the world around us, can we work in happiness and tolerance. Then we no longer need to impress others and to prove that we are better than they, whether in body, mind, soul, or spirit. But we can then, indeed, work side by side with them for the coming of the Kingdom, which is the presence of Christ in the world. Remember, there is only one Christ and that is the universal Christ; not merely Jesus who lived two thousand years ago, who could easily be reduced to a charismatic figure who lived a long time ago, had remarkable gifts, and died a most tragic death. I believe this, but it is a completely inadequate description of the full Christ.

The full Christ is the perfectly formed human being; the type of human being that I described a little while before who shows in himself what it is to be a fulfilled individual, no longer isolated and proving himself better than others, but one so self-giving that his life is one of universal blessing and everyone in his presence is now changed. This is the great promise: you will be changed (1 Corinthians 15.51; 2 Corinthians 3.18).

That which was not present before, now will be there. A new person will come into our lives. This change, which is the promise of the Christian life, comes when we are in Christ, no longer mere individuals proving that we are special, but now completely in Christ in the form of love. This is our hope as we grow on into the nature of the Lord Jesus. That is what it is to be a Christian; no longer an isolated individual who may have charismatic gifts, but now one fully in Christ whose love permeates the world, and from whom love pours out to the world, bringing all things through Christ to the nature of God who is reality, for God is love and in that love we were all conceived. We were all conceived for what is meant for us to know in the life of the world to come.

But is all this merely a pipe-dream, a tragic delusion? It is here where doubt is vitally important, for only in playing its part in the world's current affairs, may we bring the vision to life. Doubt ceases to be merely a negative attitude to the future when we all rise silently and do the work set ahead of us by providence, but we must not drown our caution in ill-conceived fanaticism or charismatic zeal.

# 8 Doubt and the moral order

An especially limiting feature of the standing order of morality, by which I mean the study and the subsequent practice of the choices of right and wrong, is the effect it has on our lives. This may be assessed not so much by how we feel, as by how our presence affects other people. We may, for instance, effect an air of *bonhomie* sufficient to convince those who believe that they know us quite well, while in fact a cloud might separate us quite sharply from them. This is not so much the cloud of unknowing about which the medieval mystic wrote, as the far less separative cloud of common decency that may form a distinct barrier between us and them. This barrier of dubious activity and our way of evading its results serve to sully the moral order. The situation was well summarized by Miguel de Unamuno (1864–1937), a hero for the forces of common decency during the Spanish Civil War during the 1930s. He wrote 'Faith which does not doubt is dead faith'. This is spelled out even more explicitly: 'Cure yourself of the inclination to bother about how you look to other people. Be concerned only with the idea God has of you.' The first quotation of Unamuno contains the vital paradox of doubt: if you are quite sure you are infallibly right, there is something radically wrong with your clear understanding of reality. Take the dogmatic medical practitioner, for example, who can only pity practitioners of alternative medicine, or the self-assured psychiatrist who is arrogantly convinced that all mental illness stems from internal sources. Such a practitioner will not so much as glanc at the possibility that behavioural disorders may from time to time have a psychic background, by which I mean that there may be interference from entities, both living and discarnate, which infest and invade the minds of those suffering from intrinsic mental disorder and cause further confusion and terror.

On the more material level, we encounter the dogmatic politician whose assessment of the state of the world or of their country is amusingly, yet horrifyingly, naïve, through personal prejudice and sheer ignorance.

Ignorance is much more than merely the basis of destructive doubt, inasmuch as, more than any other emotional state, when prejudice has occluded the sight of a well-qualified, professional worker in the fields of national or international affairs, it clouds the mind. Religion and the scientific world outlook are both inimical to the sight-denying capacity of doubt. The first is essentially a scheme of reality which has been devised by the arrogant human mind determined to impress itself on its fellow human beings that they may believe what is scarcely credible to effect power over human thought, or select a sacerdotal caste or class that may be able to assert absolute power over the independent ability of humans to judge for themselves what is right and wholesome and what is wrong and ill-considered. The second worships perpetually at the altar of reason in an exclusive company: science is its god.

Of all the human institutions, the Church, using the term in its widest meaning to include all religious agencies, should be the way forward to a decent society with fairness, honesty, and purity of action, whether sexual, financial, or political, as the real test of innocent motive to a service that the whole world can see. It claims allegiance to a power that transcends human understanding and whose nature is love, wisdom, and compassion. Love is a total self-giving to the limits of wisdom, for what use is my sacrifice if it cannot be used valuably by the person to whom it is given? Compassion is an ardent feeling for the suffering of another person or persons. Love acts to its maximal degree when it is geared to its height, we know that we have crossed over from death to life, because we love our fellow-Christians. This famous passage from 1 John 3.14 gives an admirably lucid account of the new life of love seen in the person of Jesus Christ. It is also grossly inadequate in that it limits the institution of love to a special group, great no doubt, but still merely one of many individuals humbly doing their work with us, while on earth. Judaism is a religion of wisdom, no surprise when one considers the brilliance of the Jews over many generations. Their mystical outflow is poorly generated when compared with the great religions of the East, especially Buddhism and Hinduism. Islam resembles Judaism with regard to its reverence for the Bible, and its respect for its own teaching in the Koran; and the finest Muslim teachers have emphasized the need for its teaching to be revised in the confrontation of new knowledge that reveals itself constantly in the greater world than its own limited field. Islam also has a beautiful mystic content in the form of Sufism with its emphasis on love.

All this is excellent, of course, and little can be faulted but, in fact, few of its practitioners have practised what they have preached. All believe that they are right; they are not so much ignorant as arrogant, and in that arrogance they are not really prepared to listen to anything other than their own views. The moral order teaches us that of ourselves we know very little. It is only when we relate positively and constructively with other people that we are able to move beyond our own selfishness to an understanding of reality that can embrace all people and all forms of life, and then we can begin to appreciate the brilliance of the generations that have come from Jews, Hindus, Buddhists, Muslims and others: also, so that we may all grow into that fullness of being that was shown absolutely in the total Christ. I have already emphasized that the total Christ is more than a single person. His nature was shown in a single person, of that I have no doubt at all, but his basis is in all people who are prepared to go beyond themselves and give of themselves fully to all the world and to all life. In this way they grow into the fullness of life, which is the basis of all our common humanity.

When we feel that we know everything according to some written text, we invariably twist our own understanding and our relationships with other people, and become more and more offensive and ignorant. This is the tragedy of the moral order when it is seen solely on a dogmatic level. The moral order is good when it can be changed. In other words, there is no definite or infinite moral order. When I start to tell you what is good and what is bad, and what you should do and what you should not do, I immediately fill you with my own prejudices.

What is the right way to live? Jesus said 'You shall love your neighbour as yourself'. Indeed, this comes from the Bible even before Jesus (Leviticus 19.18). The actual moral order is very simple; it is contained in the Ten Commandments, in the Sermon on the Mount and the rather similar teachings in the other great religious traditions also. But if I were to set out to tell you what to do, and gave you a written script, I would immediately cramp your style, and in the end you would cease to be a full, real human being.

What is the right way to live your life? Is chastity better than promiscuity, for instance? On one level the answer must be 'Yes'. Nearly everybody would agree that a chaste lifestyle is to be preferred to one of sexual promiscuity. Yet if you look at the great figures of the Bible and the Koran and other sacred texts, you will find that this is not always the case. Something often seems to be missing from strict morality, and that is love. If I can give my love to you, even in terms of bodily action, I may be closer to God than if I restrict myself from you and will not give fully of myself to you and what you need.

Is it better to steal or to remain absolutely perfect in one's honesty? Again, it depends on the situation. If one is stealing in order to give food to a starving child, it can be justified. On the other hand, if one steals merely out of greed, the action is indubitably wrong. In other words, the moral order cannot simply be defined unilaterally and categorically without reference to its final point of application. If we were living in a perfect world, those who lived perfectly on a moral level would be the ones to follow, but in the world we live in, with so many distortions of morality, even produced by people who seem on the surface to be the very paragons of the right way of living, they should have doubts about their own actions.

What about those who are involved in shady dealings on the Stock Exchange, and are dishonest in their material lives as well? And yet they may at times be much closer to the naked truth about themselves than many others who are able to make a good impression on other people. I am not suggesting here that it is a good thing to be immoral or in any way dishonest in one's dealings: that could not surely be right, but there are times when giving oneself in one's emptiness to other people may be much nearer the heart of true charity than merely keeping it for oneself in a hard-hearted, cruel sort of way.

Doubt is at the very heart of the moral order. Decisions may be very easy for those who know what is right and what is wrong, for they are satisfied both with themselves and what they have. They have no needs any more, whether it is in the field of personal relationships or in relation to money or other possessions that they might want. But there are others who need things that they may not have: beauty, joy, acceptance; they too need to have something the world cannot give them, and until they have it, they will never know what it is to be fulfilled individuals.

Thus, while it is right that Unamuno should say that 'Faith which does not doubt is dead faith', dead faith is so bound to assurance that it does not need to move on at all; it knows that it is right and can just go to sleep. That is the nature of so much religion: I have fulfilled my duties for today, therefore I have nothing further to do. Only when my faith is alive, only then is my doubt truly alive, can I start having a living faith, and that faith may enliven my doubt and then I might start to live consciously.

This is something we need to consider again towards the

end of this book, when we come to our good fellow traveller, Job, who was such a fine, righteous man until tragedy smote him and he had to begin to live and see life as it really was and could no longer rest behind prosperity of one kind or another.

To my mind there is no question but that the tragedies of one kind or another which smash us and make us fit for nothing are a way of growth towards not only our knowledge of God, but our love of our fellow creatures also. When all goes well for us, we become increasingly smug and sure of ourselves, and also rather superstitious inasmuch as, should we do anything wrong, something unpleasant may befall us, and so we lose that lust for life which is the basis of all creative human existence.

It is a strange paradox that when we do something well, we may be nearer the dark side of reality than when we have moved beyond the bright side and are now in the darkness itself; through the darkness a greater light may shine, but when we are asleep we are incapable of seeing anything at all. This is why a great deal of what might be called conventional or orthodox religion is so dead. It is not because its teaching is dead, but because its practitioners are dead. They are so sure of themselves, so closed to anyone else that they do not know what they are doing or what they are seeing. Fortunately, there may be a later opening to the Divine Presence, and through this to the world around them.

If we are in a state of prosperity, we often do not know this rejoicing, but instead we quarrel with one another. If we are in a beautiful garden we are often blind to the beauty, and see only the dirt on the grass, if anything at all. Only when an illness comes to us may we understand what health is about, and then at last we begin to work towards bodily soundness. Fortunately for us there is never an end to the munificence of God, even when we have wasted and spoiled the gifts which he has given us.

Life is the most marvellous gift in the world to us because it is vibrant with activity. We do not have to imagine anything at all, we just have to be still and listen intently.

The more we try and harmonize with it, the more we put it from us. Just as the more I try to prove I agree with you, the more obvious it becomes that I am not really sympathetic to you at all, but am trying to make the most favourable impression on you. One simply should be quiet, still, and listen, and in that state joy comes to one, and one begins to know that God is there, and one begins to know who God is as well: not a person, nor a being, nor a state of awareness; in fact, the only way that I could define God is purely negatively, as the great mystics have always told us. 'Not this, not that' is how the Hindu puts it. 'The cloud of unknowing' is another way of putting it. God is always known by the negativity of his presence. And yet in that negativity we are closer to his being than we would be if he poured out a shower of wonderful events which blinded us by their dazzling quality.

'Neither this, neither that', the Buddhists say of God, in whom they do not believe in at all as a personal entity, but as emptiness or the great void. How hard it is for a Westerner to see ultimate reality in those terms! But then, it is perfectly true; it is much more real than visualizing God as a person who shows favouritism towards a group of people whom he likes especially, and is very angry with others whom he intends to punish if they do not do exactly what he wants of them.

What about the punishing nature of God, then? Does God punish? Is there any moral order at all? We believe there is a moral order, because without it human beings could not live as moral beings, and they would destroy each other. But it is not God that does the destroying; God is quiet, and when we are in the stillness too, we begin to see what we ought to be doing, and then we know God as the supreme providence which guides everything by his very presence. He does not need to shout, command, or produce effects of one type or another in order to make us sit up and be aware. He simply tells us to be quiet, be still, and know that he is God (Psalm 46.10). In that stillness we know of the presence of God, the God who destroyed the enemies of the Jews in this famous psalm; it was not God that was destroying them, it was they who were destroying themselves because they did not practise stillness, and therefore fell foul of their adversaries and precipitated their own destruction. When we begin to know stillness, we can begin to know the power of God in the form of eternal silence, a silence that is more eloquent than speaking for millions of years.

How strange it is that the nature of reality is known in its negative form, the way of negativity, the cloud of unknowing! When we know this, we know something about reality, and then we can begin to see what God is telling us about the nature of reality as well. That is the way that we can be aware of God if we are sensitive. We cannot know him directly. If we did know God, he might burn us up! This is one way of seeing him. More likely, we would be swallowed up into a void of sheer non-being. Neither of these views is very frightening from my point of view, but they are unsatisfactory because they are negative. But when we know the nature of God, we are still, quiet, and begin to listen. God does not need my stillness, but other people do. It is only when I can be quiet and listen that I can hear what other people are saying, and therefore can be of some help to them according to their need.

Most people are of no help to others at all, because they are not really listening. They want to help; it is not that they are not concerned, but their real concern is for themselves and what other people are thinking about them. Only when they have moved beyond self-concern and all its egoism can they know the other person, and be of help as they ought to be. That is the way in which we know God. When we are quiet, a presence of stillness comes to us and at last we know the true God who brings us close to the love of our fellow creatures, not only human beings, but everything that lives. All are part of the essential beauty of the world. Nothing is hidden from us. But unfortunately, we are usually so full of ourselves and our own concerns that the beauty of the world and its glory are largely hidden from us, and we are not able to see anything at all of it.

That is what the moral order is basically about. It is not

being very good or doing the right thing, or following a code of laws like the Ten Commandments, the Sermon on the Mount, or any other great teaching, excellent as all these are. But they are all essentially of human origin in the end. I would say that even about the Sermon on the Mount or the Ten Commandments; they are wonderful prescriptions of the positive way of life, but they do not get you very far until you are still, and can begin to assimilate and practise them.

The greatest of all these prescriptions is surely the Sermon on the Mount, but how can you follow it? I asked this question in one of the earlier chapters of this book. If you are slapped on the right cheek, turn the left cheek to be slapped as well. If a person takes money from you, let them have more of it. How can you do this? It is really idealistic, but nobody could quarrel with its beauty. The answer is, do not become attached to material things at all; while you are attached to material things, there must be problems in your life; material things are illusions. Here I am today, a man growing in age, rather crippled as I have said before, in due course I may or may not get better or worse; but one thing is certain, I am going to die, as everyone else does. Everything that we have here is an illusion. The Hindus speak about *maya* – illusion. While we are attached to anything in this life, it goes from us through the process of time, the attenuating process of time by which we all live.

Without death nothing would live at all, because there would be such an overcrowding in the world that nobody would be able to move. That is why death is possibly God's greatest gift to all of us. But it should be a death after a constructive life when we have seen and enjoyed the wonders around us; and have been able to give of our particular genius to other people. Then when the time comes for us to pass on, we will not only have seen and understood what we have been given, but will be able to give to other people as well, and joy will come to all of us through that meeting. This is the spiritual way of life and the moral order.

Use everything that you have been given properly and

advantageously. Thank God for it all, and give it to other people; do not cling on to anything. The tendency to hang on to things is one of our greatest human foibles. Remember Mary of Magdala and the other woman, and the risen Christ: they clasped his feet, and he told them to take word to his brothers, to go ahead and leave and see him in Galilee (Matthew 28.6–10). 'Do not cling to me', said Jesus, 'for I have not yet ascended to the Father. But go to my brothers and tell them that I am ascending to my Father and your Father, to my God and your God' (John 20.17).

The full meaning of this is somewhat obscure, but one thing is certain, we dare not cling to any being while that being is still with us. That being has to move on. Had the women really stayed with Jesus and not left him, they would not have moved on themselves, and would have been attached to an entity or an appearance that would not let them go. When we have to face the fact of death, do not let us be too lugubrious about it. Let us see that it is our way forward to a new existence. This applies to all people. It is we who make death a tragedy, by clinging on to earthly life desperately, and not seeing what God is telling us about reality. The moral order is here to tell us that nothing in this world belongs to us. It is here for our experimentation and our experience, and after this we are fitted to go on to other things, notably to quit our present home and to be with other entities. The real life that is the life here is the life of the spirit, in which we may know God, as the silent being in whom all things exist. That is how all mystics understand God. He is silence, absolute silence, but in that silence there is a greater presence of being than in all the noise that human beings can create.

Be still and know that I am God (Psalm 46.10). This is the God who sustains us by his loving presence. He does not interfere in our lives. He is there to support us by his concern and loving care. He does not do anything deleteriously to any other creature because all creatures are under his protective wing. The very statement: Be still and know that I am God, is actually something of a mistranslation. A more acceptable version is 'Let be then; learn that I am God' (46.10).

The Psalms often stress the close link between God's chosen people Israel, but in many of the finest of them the Lord of Hosts has a universal character. Of course, God loves everything that he has made and there is nothing outside the moral order, because through that order we come to be responsible human beings, whatever we may call ourselves in terms of nation, race, religion, colour, or creed. Unfortunately we all tend to identify ourselves according to these criteria, and the results can be destructive, as we all know only too well.

God has no favourites. We learn that from the conversion of Cornelius to Christianity by Peter (Acts 10.34–35). God loves everything that he has made, and there are no degrees of love. You either love or else you do not love, but you cannot love some people more than others. This is one of the things that we humans do not understand properly. If I say that I love you, I love you with all my heart, and soul, and mind and strength: not only with a little piece of myself. Unfortunately again, most of us do not see this clearly, we have a sort of Laodicean (lukewarm) view of relationships, and are prepared to give what we want to give but no more. In the end, we have to learn that all that is created is created through the love of God whom nobody has ever seen visually. But in that love all are brought into his presence.

As a created being I am of very little worth. What am I but a mass of flesh and bones here today, gone tomorrow! But in my mind, in my mental and spiritual capacity, I am of incalculable value. Furthermore I am now small compared with what I shall be eventually; again not on a material level but on a spiritual level. Consider the really great creators of humanity, the musicians, artists, and writers and all the others of that type who have inspired humanity to a new understanding of what it should mean to be a human: no longer fighting against each other, or acquiring wealth, or becoming richer or more powerful, but simply giving to others the products of the inspiration with which they have been endowed.

If you are an inspirational person, as I am myself, you do not need to grasp for inspiration; it comes to you quite spontaneously. When you are quiet and still, the idea comes to you and the form comes with it as well. I am sure that this applies with far greater intent to the really great musicians, writers, and artists of the world; they are open, the idea comes to them, and it develops into a marvellous creation, which they in turn can bequeath to the rest of humanity.

There is no greater gift than that of creativity. It cannot be bargained for, nor can you work towards it. For as soon as you do this, the ego intrudes and whatever is formed is spoiled. If there is one thing that prevents creativity, it is egoism. Even now, if I were to speak to you from an egotistical standpoint, I would get in the way, the creative process would be abolished, and anything regarding the Holy Spirit would be totally obliterated. You would simply hear my opinions, with which you may or may not agree, but in the end you would become disgruntled and bored. I of myself have nothing to offer at all. I know that perfectly well. This is certainly not false modesty, I can assure you; it is simply common sense and a realistic attitude to life.

In fact I have got a great deal to offer, my whole life is there before you if you want it, but if you were to pump it out of me, or I were to give it to you spontaneously, it would soon become embarrassing and boring. The real life is the life that you can see in me, and you can find in me as you hear me speak; then you can begin to know something about me, my attitude to life, and more important than that, what life has done to me and what life does to a human being generally; then you are beginning to learn something that could be of value to you. I, as it were, am a mere catalyst then. I do not change, but I am part of the spiritual process that brings life into full being for you. But as soon as I get in the way, I become a god in my own right and the results are not attractive, to put it mildly.

The moral order is one in which we are close to God in doing the work that he wants us to do. It is not being moral in terms of doing the right thing as opposed to the wrong thing. So often in the history of the world the right thing has been tyrannical, while the wrong thing has been the basis of a new creativity. Many of the greatest artists have been regarded as immoral and disgusting, yet they have been the founders of a new understanding of relationships. William Blake in the eighteenth century and our own contemporary artist Francis Bacon are classical examples of people who have, in one way or another, been regarded as unpleasant if not disgusting and repulsive, and yet they have given us a closer view of reality than merely that of the staid, complacent writers and artists of the past. Which writers of the past would you be particularly interested in? Surely those like Dickens and Thackeray and others who have given us a frank description of life as it was lived in the last century. The Dickensian view of life was not particularly pleasant, because life in mid-nineteenth-century England was not pleasant for the broad masses. But people who have written in accordance with their smug view or understanding have irritated us, and not in any way lifted the net higher over the human situation.

The moral order, in other words, is an indication of the human situation as it is now. It may not be particularly pleasant, but it gives one a fairly accurate indication of how we live and what our attitudes to life are. It is far better to have an honest assessment of the moral order, which may not be particularly attractive, than to say and do the right things and to know the right people, while we ourselves are dishonest in our dealings with other people on a deeper level. And this dishonesty may not be direct fraudulence; it may be simply adopting ignorant attitudes which are foreign to us. Jesus said things that must have horrified many people in his time, and yet today he is an exemplar of a morality which can never wane.

Look how he described the religious authorities of his time in Matthew 23.

Jesus then addressed the people and his disciples in these words: 'The doctors of the law and the Pharisees sit in the chair of Moses, therefore do what they tell you, pay attention to their words, but do not follow their practice, for they say one thing and do another. They make up heavy loads and pile them on the shoulders of others but will not themselves lift a finger to ease the burden. Whatever they do is done for show. They go about wearing broad phylacteries and with large tassels on their robes; they love to have the places of honour at feasts and the chief seats in synagogues, to be greeted respectfully in the streets and to be addressed as "rabbi".

'But you must not be called "rabbi", for you have one Rabbi and you are all brothers. Do not call anyone on earth "father", for you have one Father and he is in heaven. Nor must you be called "teacher"; you have one Teacher, the Messiah. The greatest among you must be your servant. Whoever exalts himself will be humbled; and whoever humbles himself will be exalted. Alas for you, scribes and Pharisees, hypocrites! You shut the door of the Kingdom of Heaven in people's faces, you do not enter yourselves, and when others try to enter, you stop them. Alas for you, scribes and Pharisees, hypocrites! You travel over sea and land to win one convert; and when you have succeeded you make him twice as fit for hell as you are yourselves.

'Alas for you, blind guides! You say, "If someone swears by the sanctuary, that is nothing, but if he swears by the gold in the sanctuary he is bound by his oath." Blind fools! Which is the more important, the gold or the sanctuary that sanctifies the gold? Or you say, "If someone swears by the altar, that is nothing; but if he swears by the offering that lies on the altar, he is bound by his oath." What blindness! Which is the more important, the offering, or the altar which sanctifies it? To swear by the altar, then, is to swear both by the altar and by whatever lies on it; to swear by the sanctuary is to swear both by the sanctuary and by him who dwells there; and to swear by Heaven is to swear both by the throne of God and by Him who sits upon it.

'Alas for you scribes and Pharisees, hypocrites! You pay tithes of mint and dill and cummin, but you have overlooked the weightier demands of the law – justice, mercy, and good faith. It is these you should have practised without neglecting the others. Blind guides! You strain off a midge, yet gulp down a camel! Alas for you, scribes and Pharisees, hypocrites! You clean the outside of a cup or a dish, and leave the inside full of greed and self-indulgence. Blind Pharisee! Clean the inside of the cup first; then the outside will be clean also.' (Matthew 23.1–26)

These are stern words; they are based on religious hypocrisy on a large scale. The terrible thing about it all is that the people whom Jesus condemned so vehemently were completely ignorant of their hypocrisy; they believed that if they performed certain ritual actions all would be well. They did not see that if their inner attitude was wrong, their outer action would be fruitless. So much religion of the past has been based on this inner hypocrisy, which is really an indication of ignorance and superstition.

Only if one has done the right thing first, as Jesus says, can subsidiary things be right. Therefore, before you eat say your prayers and your grace devoutly, then you can eat well and what you eat will be blessed. Saying grace is a way of thanking God before you have food to eat at all. It is a wonderful custom, but it must be said with intent, then the moral order is inside you; where you eat is blessed with the moral order also.

# 9 The Sacrament of the Present Moment

The Sacrament of the Present Moment: this phrase, used by Jean Pierre de Caussade in his famous classic *Self-Abandonment to the Divine Providence*, tells us that we have to be open to life in the present moment at all times. Abandon yourself to the present moment and all that it contains, let your mind be aware and clear and not clogged by debris that prevents you not merely thinking, but actually focusing properly. We know God when we are quiet and still, and we are open to his embrace. We do not know him when we are full of our own thoughts and worries of one type or another. The self-abandonment to the Divine Providence is openness to the present moment. This present moment may be a very pleasant moment, or it may be a very threatening one.

Sometimes unpleasant things happen to us out of the blue, and sometimes we are thrilled by the wonders of grace that come to us day by day and moment by moment. But one thing is certain; we have to steel ourselves to what is given to us at that particular moment, and learn from it. Self-abandonment to the Divine Providence means giving of ourselves fully to God as he shows himself to us now with all the glories at hand as well. Then we can begin to live as we ought to live, and thoughts of a merely egoistical level pale into the background and eventually dissolve into thin air.

The self-abandonment of which de Caussade spoke is giving of ourselves fully to God in the present moment. To be aware of him in the hush of quietness when there is no thought, no speculation of any type at all, only quietness and availability, is the way in which we know the presence of God. We cannot know God by thinking about him, as the passage in the *Cloud of Unknowing* has already reminded us: 'By love may he be gotten and holden but by thought never.'

But how do you love? – this is the problem here. If I tell you to start loving your neighbour, as indeed you will find prescribed both in the New and the Old Testaments, you will end up absolutely frustrated. Love cannot be manufactured or evoked. The more I try to love you, the more hypocritical my affection will appear. If I really want to love you – and I should certainly want to love everybody – I have to put myself at ease. Egoism has to go completely, and I have to be quiet before the essence of reality. Putting self before all else is a certain way of not knowing what love is about. But if I can begin to put self behind me, then love will come in front of me, and I can start to love, primarily myself, for we must love ourselves before we can love other people. Our love then goes to other people as well, as it grows in ourself, but until it is firmly rooted in ourself, it will remain unstable in other people.

Remember the first and second commandments: 'Thou shalt love the Lord thy God with all thy heart and with all thy soul and with all thy strength' (Deuteronomy 6.5) and the second which is like unto it; 'Thou shalt love thy neighbour as thyself' (Leviticus 19.18). The love of God is extremely exalting, even if rather impossible for most of us to attain. The love of self seems so selfish that it almost has wrong connotations about it, but if we do not love ourselves, we cannot love our neighbour and we cannot love anybody else either. In fact, both are equally important. We should start by loving God and our neighbour, but we should end by loving ourselves and everybody else as well. Love is of universal sympathy and nobody can be outside its orbit if they are to do the work that God has prepared for them to do. Self-abandonment to Divine Providence, about which de Caussade writes, is basically giving ourselves and everyone else to God, but primarily ourselves. And when we have given ourselves to the Divine Providence, to the love of God, we will be shown the way to love our fellow creatures and also those whom we intuitively dislike.

Anyone involved in psychical studies will realize that there are some people who are not very pleasant, and we have to face the fact that in any of our lives there are moments when we ourselves are quite repulsive. This cannot in any way be obviated or expunged by pretending it does not really exist. What is there cannot be merely wished away. Ultimately, that which is unclean or unpleasant in your mind has to be dedicated to God in complete trust and quietness. Eventually you and that from which or whom you diverge may unite and form a common base. This is the only way in which you can begin to form a relationship with someone whom you intuitively dislike. The intuition may have had very good grounds. It may have been based on something very unpleasant in the past, perhaps long ago, but I would not for one moment advise that you should abandon it, but eventually it should be transcended.

This is the only way in which love can ultimately govern our universe; it cannot be done by an act of the will. The more you try to transcend it by pretending that it does not really exist, or that it is something which you ought to have outgrown long ago, the more it will not move one iota. But if you are quiet, something deeper than you will come and form a pleasant veil over the darkness. And soon light will appear and bring it all to the light. It is only through the light that the darkness is brought up to God and its noxious element ceases to worry you. While we try to escape from our own concerns and will not face our own problems, we cannot know God or our fellow creatures.

Self-knowledge is crucially important, and we should not be ashamed of ourselves if what we find is not particularly pleasant. The same applies to everybody else. None of us here is a particularly pleasant individual. There are saints amongst us undoubtedly; most of us are pretty ordinary folk, and a few are quite unpleasant, but in the end we all are children of God, and we can all be still and quiet and above all not cling on to the things of this world. Then we can move beyond distrust and into a state of rest and quietude. If I have a considerable amount of money or other possessions and I do not trust you, I will never be really easy in your company. If I had a secret which I did not trust you to keep and you knew it, again I would not be relaxed in your company.

But we should have no secrets, for all is of God and all that we have should be acknowledged of God as well. It is only then that we can be completely quiet and happy, but if we are trying to hide something from anyone, or trying to conceal our innermost thoughts, we will never really be at rest. This is not the way of spirituality. This is the way of inquietude and unrest without any semblance of love.

As long as I remember you as a person of ill repute, I will distrust you and get as far away from you as possible. When I remember you as a person of no conspicuous repute at all, I will simply dismiss you from my concern and not think too much about you. This does not get us very far on the path of positive relationship either.

But when I am able to remember you as a friend, then I can trust you. To be a friend does not necessarily require passionate love; it needs simply to trust a person and to be happy in their company. You can only do this when you have nothing to hide from a person and can be quiet in front of them. Then your doubt becomes one of faith because there is nothing to hide any more.

In fact, doubt and hiding come very close together in this scheme of understanding. The more I doubt, the more I will tend to hide; the more faith I have, the more I can reveal of myself to other people, and the less do I care whether they share my secrets or betray them to other people. It ultimately does not matter. The only thing that matters is to do my work properly and with as much love, caring, and solicitude as possible. Then, whether people like me or not becomes increasingly irrelevant. But if I have to put on a brave face and show myself to be superior to others, I can only know that I am really inferior, and in that state of inferiority, I will be in unhappiness and misery also. Therefore, self-abandonment to the Divine Providence is the only way of coming to a knowledge of God and a knowledge of his ways of working among us also. Remember always that nobody has ever seen God, and that God is known by his effect on our being rather than on any relationship that we have had on a level of sensation.

How do I know God? Certainly not by any outer manifestation, only by an inner change in my consciousness. That is the way that a mystic knows God. This is the way in which you may be able to explain God to an arrogant agnostic. They will never have seen God, because God is not visible. But they will see themselves in relationship to God, and what they see may not be at all pleasant. On the other hand, they may thank God when an act of tremendous grace occurs in their life, which changes the whole basis of their understanding of reality.

When a person who believed that they were mortally ill suddenly gets better, or someone in the throes of despair suddenly moves into a state of happiness again, they know the workings of God in their life, and that God is the God who is the creator of all things, particularly themselves through their misery into their strength and goodness. It is in this way that we know how God exists in our life and shows himself. He is indeed a living God, one who lives in us and through us; he lives in other people as well. He is no longer merely a figment of our imagination, but the very basis of our life through whom we can start to do the things that we ought to be doing and showing others what they ought to be doing also. Thus God is a living God, in that he produces life in the world, in us, and in all people.

Numerous people wonder whether the resurrection of Jesus actually occurred, and there are many doubters who feel that it may or may not have happened. In the end, nobody alive at present has seen the resurrection of Our Lord. You may or may not believe, according to your own feeling, but one thing is obvious: those who did know Jesus when he was alive, and met him afterwards in his resurrection form, were changed as individuals. That for me is the positive proof of the resurrection of Jesus. I am not nearly so convinced about the resurrection appearances as by his weak disciples being changed from doubting and fearful individuals to people full of joy and courage, and able to live a new life. That is the way that resurrection shows itself. And it is not only the resurrection of Jesus; it is the resurrection of all life. If I in my life can grow through doubt and unhappiness to a new understanding of reality, God in the form of the resurrected Christ is with me as well, and I can begin to live fully and bring that life to others also.

In other words, you do not need miracles to show you the way of resurrection. Indeed, miracles have often more than one mode of interpretation. It is the change in psyche of the individual that proves the resurrection, and that change can never ever be denied, because it is of the basis of reality. Only when we know this do we know the Lord is with us and that nothing in the world can separate him from us. Once you have known Jesus in this form, you know that he is always with you, and not only with you but with everyone else as well, and that through him a new life opens to the whole created universe. Now at last we begin to see what resurrection means in its fullness: not that I was dead and am now alive, but that the world was in a state of decay and has now grown into a new state of understanding of reality. This, in the form of the living Christ, is available to all people according to their own capacity to accept his new life.

If you do not want to believe in the resurrection, then you will not. There is certainly nothing that will force you to believe it. But if you are open spiritually, you will see more and more for yourself, and the evidence will grow in clarity and veracity. That is the way forward to an understanding of the mysteries of our faith; not through the eyes or the other senses, but through intuition; that same intuition that governs our knowledge of love when we are involved with people who are now dead and yet are closer to us than they ever were when they were still in our world.

I spoke about this, in Chapter 6, when I was thinking about how marvellous things occur through the enigma of

God, and we are able to receive him in our state of present disillusionment. But the real God does not simply give us things; he gives us his presence so that we can be with him in one total universe; and one total Christ can take over the whole created universe, not only humans or even animals, but everything that exists, and then a new life comes to us and to everyone, as we begin to see how he works in our own life and how he changes us from glory to glory.

The Sacrament of the Present Moment finds its fruition at the moment of death, when we will confront the life we led on earth and have to come to terms with our various attitudes and attributes, while we were there. Now we are obliged to face our past life in terms of our present relationships. Destruction is the end of our physical bodies, and then we have to face our indeterminate future in an obscure after-life state. St Paul puts it thus in Galatians 6.7–8: 'Make no mistake about this: God is not to be fooled; everyone reaps what he sows. If he sows in a field of his own spiritual nature, he will reap from it a harvest of corruption; but if he sows in a field of the Spirit he will reap from it a harvest of eternal life.'

The physical body has a limited duration of life; this is why the manner in which we live in the present moment is so important; for what we do in even a moment may determine our future life and that of many other people also. I personally believe in the immortality of the soul, as part of one's personality, where one's moral judgements are made and one's sense of perfection in beauty, truth, and love emanate. But physical death and destruction of all that is beautiful in our lives are unavoidable. This has a final purpose; we must not cling on to any object or personal relationship, beautiful as it may be. God is our eternal home, where all that is beautiful and treasurable here prepares us for eating and drinking the body and blood of Christ, in his everlasting home. He is the Sacrament of the Present Moment, and in him all life is transfigured into an eternal sacrament. This is the Sacrament of the Present Moment in our lives.

# 10 Anguish

Anguish is the most terrible state you may experience because everything that you have held on to, every hope that may have sustained you, has now left and there is nothing but complete disintegration. Anybody who is a person has to undergo the experience of anguish. It may be the death of a child, or someone they have loved very much. It may be the destruction of their family, or the failure of their hopes, or their country or the whole world. We all have to know that nothing on a material level can be relied on permanently. In the end, nothing we know on the level of relationships can survive for any length of time.

Anguish is the experience of severe bodily and mental pain: that we are nothing; the world is nothing; all on which we anchored our hopes is also nothing. This is important, because it takes our mind fully away from the things of this world and their pleasures. We have to move beyond childish and childlike attitudes to the adult way which is a way of ultimate being.

Until you have experienced anguish you have not lived your full, proper life. It is a situation of complete desperation, both physical and mental, and nothing that you believed in before seems to have any relevance to your present state, gloom or despair. What is the essential difference between desperation and despair? Desperation is a state in which you hang on for grim death to the one thing you think will help you in your present state of emptiness. Despair is a complete hopelessness that there is nothing at all in the world, and there is nothing for you to do but to give up. Therefore, desperation at least holds out the possibility that there may be one remedy to help you in your present state of negativity, while despair denies you that possibility. The ultimate end of unalleviated despair is quite obviously suicide. On the other hand, desperation tells you inwardly that there is something to be hoped for, and that you will not commit suicide, unless you are a very gloomy person. You will hold on, even by a hair's breadth, and through this, follow through to greater things in the future. It is very good to experience desperation. Then at last you have to face things directly as they really are and not behind the veil of illusion. Not many people can do this, and most people who surround a person in a state of desperation are remarkably useless. Most of them run a mile, because they know their own inadequacy and cannot face your inadequacy either. In a state of despair nothing can prevail.

Is there any hope for a person in a state of despair? I believe there is. This is the presence of God. It cannot be worked out intellectually, but if you are in a state of despair and everything you believed or held on to has proved to be an illusion, learn to be quiet. The mind and its clamouring chatter certainly cannot help you in this situation. But if you are quiet, a way may open to you which will show you that despair was itself an illusion, and a much greater reality lay ahead of you if only you could have glimpsed your own state of rather selfish unhappiness.

That was the situation with Job. Once everything had been taken from him, he had nothing to do but anticipate, and rather look forward to, death. But he stayed the course and was ultimately saved. We shall consider Job again in the next chapter. The point about anguish is that it teaches us that we have to know more and more about ourselves and to depend less and less on other people, in terms of the help they may give us. I am not saying from this that other people are unimportant, but what I am saying is that they are useless to us when we are in a state of hopelessness, and have lost our bearings. They do not know either us, or more importantly themselves either. This applies as much to those who follow a religion of one type or another as to those who depend entirely on the power of the human mind. Only when we know nothing, may we come to see despair itself and the anguish it causes as the way to our knowledge of God. The mind can never know God. I have said this on a number of occasions already. God may be known by love but never by thought. There are two types of God that are registered by the mind. First, the God of the real religion, who shows himself to us, and we know of his presence by the fact that he is a living god, and one who can converse with us through our own being. He does not converse by speaking to us, but by opening our minds to a greater reality. The other God, very popular in the seventeenth and eighteenth centuries, was what was called the god of natural religion, or 'deism'. It was a god conjured up by the human mind to explain the mechanism of the universe. Noteworthy deists were Isaac Newton and John Locke, neither of whom could be called Christian in any meaningful sense of the word, but they could plausibly explain the existence of things by believing in a being who could create. Deism leads straight on to atheism unless one is sensible enough to see that the god of deism is a mere mechanism created by the human mind to explain the mysteries of the world, which it cannot understand in any other way. That is why this kind of god is ultimately the god of meaninglessness in human relations, one without love or compassion.

Only when we see these things clearly can we begin to understand what God is like. That is why you can try quite fruitlessly to prove the existence of God through his creation, for proof is ultimately inadequate because so much of creation is cruel, pointless, and very savage, at least intrinsically. Obviously, the type of God with whom Job conversed could not possibly have given him the answer to his problems. But through being still a new awareness came to him and God spoke to him directly, challenging him, and showing him the marvels of creation.

The marvels of creation do not depend on what we can see and hear outwardly, but on what we can see and hear on an inner level, and know as part of our own being. This is why the proof of Jesus in terms of his miracles is so inadequate. Conjurors, magicians, and charismatics can all on occasions produce effects of this type quite astonishingly. I am not saying that these people are to be summarily dismissed, but that none is of the nature of God. He lifts you up on to a higher level, and you see life in terms of Divine creativity, and you will understand how God's spirit sanctifies his works; a true miracle. Even now, if I could produce a marvel in front of you all, and it was a genuine phenomenon and not just what passes as sleight-of-hand, that would not give you any understanding of God. It would, at most, show you simply that I was a very remarkable person and that I could do things that other people could not. But this would not be the God of our Lord Jesus Christ. Only the God who moves us from our limited human understanding to ultimate reality can be the God who is the Lord of Jesus and the God of life. God sees into the depths of the human heart, and sets us free from ritualistic illusion. People in the time of Jesus demanded miracles, but they were easily deceived by anybody who had the capacity to produce something out of the ordinary. The real miracle is life itself, the human being, and their creativity. Here you get an individual who can create, doing something that makes a person real in terms of their humanity. This gives us an indication of the true quality of a miracle.

Anguish, on the other hand, shows everything that you had relied on to prove the existence of reality, to have been merely illusory: whatever you thought was the beneficent power of creation is shown to be a childish error, and has turned out to be a mistake, so that finally you can only give up hope and say there is nothing positive in life whatsoever.

Job did not reach this stage of disillusionment. He knew that creation existed. He could not possibly give an answer to the meaning of creation, let alone its suffering. The reason for this was that he was at the centre of everything he experienced, his ego demanded to be satisfied, and when this could not be done intellectually, he relinquished hope, and relapsed into despair, and then left things as they were. When we realize we are not the masters of the universe and that on our own we are very frail creatures and have very little to give, we begin to see things as they really are, and our lives can turn to face a reality in which we are important in our own right because of the individuality we have been given.

I am crucially important as an individual not because of any mental or other gifts that I may have, but because of the fact that I see things, including the universe itself, in my own particular way. The way I relate to people could be completely unique also. My relationships to others could never be mimicked by anyone else, not because they are in any way special and irreplaceable, but because they are mine, and what I can give, no matter how humble it may be, may help other people in their own lives to be and give what they ought to give. If I see myself as irreplaceable, as completely beyond any change or growth, then I am in trouble immediately. Nobody is so irreplaceable that the world cannot exist without them, for we all have something to offer, and when that has been removed from us, then we know the meaning of anguish. When I know anguish, I realize that I cease to exist as a full social being. I may still be alive in the same way as a worm might be, but the basis of my living and my creativity has been removed. It is a terrible state, and one which many people have to understand. It probably finds its fullest expression in conditions of mental disease of one type or another, particularly when the person involved does not have a complete understanding of what is going on in the mind. It is a terrifying state when our mind does not register properly, and we do not see reality in truth. Then we are in very serious trouble. Nobody is in a state of complete unapproachability. Each has their own place and we all have to pass on in due course – not merely to death, but to giving our work and lives to other people, so that they may inherit the work and we may rest and reveal ourselves in a much humbler manner. But if we cannot relinquish our task, then we suffer an increasing amount of anguish.

When I am in a state of anguish, I am in a state of egolessness; not the state that the mystic knows, but the state that the fully egoistic or human knows when their self-importance is thrust away from them, whether they like it or not, and they see only uselessness in front of them. It is essentially a state of being in which one ceases to be a recognizable member of society, but is now part of the dregs of humanity. Nobody is in any way beyond redemption, but many of us will not be able to see ourselves in another form which we would not voluntarily take upon ourselves. To be in this state of anguish is to know that all the things that we held on to with such vigour and tenacity before, even our own family and friends, are now removed from us irreversibly. It is a shocking state of desolation. Now at last we are obliged to see ourselves as we really are, no longer hidden from other people. This, indeed, is the experience of hell.

Can I ever see myself as I really am, apart from my relationships with others? That is the crucial question. If my relationship with others depends on my forcing myself on them, or depending on them, or making myself in some way irreplaceable, then I am a most unhappy individual, because all these states are illusory. But if I can be quiet, still, and give of myself, then I will never be far from positive relationships with others, and I will never know personal anguish.

Anguish can take a mental or a physical form. In physical anguish some essential function of the body fails, and we are moving close towards death. It happens inevitably after strokes and heart attacks, and with terminal cancer. Whether we are to survive or not depends not only on the medical attention we may receive, but also on our own state of being and hope so that we may proceed together with those who are helping us to a new life.

Mental and emotional anguish is related more to our understanding of our place in the world, society, and our relationships with other people. It is much more delicate and subtle, and here again our work is to learn to remain silent and not to blame God or any other supernatural power for letting us down, and wait patiently for the outcome of our dilemma. If we believe that we have a special purpose in life to fulfil, this illusion will be taken soon from us, not because it is necessarily wrong to have such a view, but because it usually means that we know what this purpose is and our self-regard gets in the way. Then we may feel that we have great potentialities in one or other form of existence, but we tend to move in the way and we cannot do what is expected of us. What is that which is expected from me? First of all, to be a reasonable and decent person, giving in such a way that others may receive knowledge of God through me. It also means helping other people to be as efficient and God-fearing as possible. To be God-fearing does not mean fearing God, but loving God and no longer clinging on to our own disposition or emancipation. None of us is indispensable, but when we see this clearly we can begin to understand what God wants us to do, and then we can stop clinging on to our own supposed indispensability, and start doing the work set out before us with proper abandon and joy as well. In other words, anguish is the negative side of joy and freedom and an understanding of God's purpose for us in life and we cannot have the one without the other. It could be extremely boring and unproductive, as well as selfish and showing a lack of understanding of the deeper issues of existence, always to be in a positive frame of mind, because we could not understand and be of assistance to an unhappy person.

Only when we can be quiet and still, and listen to the voice of God in clear silence, may we know what lies in front of us. The god of deism (natural theology) is not a living god and there is no purpose behind deism at all. This moves on inevitably towards atheism in which we can do without God entirely, and we can be a god in our own right. We know where this leads to in terms of human relationships.

But if we are to know the way of God, we have to be still and listen. We cannot dictate or in any way interpret according to our own understanding. We can only listen and be transformed. That is ultimately what religion is about: it leads on to spirituality in other words. Religion is a way of life which moves beyond our own understanding and dicta-torship of the world as we would want it, and teaches us what is real or illusory, but until we know the humility that comes through intense suffering and self-annihilation, we cannot know the way to God. Job himself had to tread this way in his path to understanding. During the latter part of the seventeenth and eighteenth centuries, the period of Enlightenment, as it is sometimes called, human beings realized that through scientific knowledge they could interpret life and the meaning of the world increasingly as they wanted and how they wanted to do it. But the result was a break in human relationships and an inevitable movement towards the dominance of the human mind, with its enormous power in research, but not unfortunately in insight, or great human sympathy. The result has been a terrible disappointment in our own lives.

Religion, in its own right, has very little to recommend it, for we all know that in terms of the history of religion, the human being soon creates a god in their own image. According to my own religion, I will interpret god according to that religion and see that my god is the only right one. So religion itself does not lead to God, but without religion we do not know God at all. The basis of religion is really that of a spiritual discipline, to keep us quiet by means of spiritual exercises, so that we may learn to move beyond ourselves, our own desires and fears, our own anguish as well as our own ecstasy, in other words, so that we may begin to know the truth that sets us free from many different illusions.

There is no truth that embraces only the intellect. If I think that my religion is the only right one, I am sure to come into conflict with others very rapidly and the results will be mutually destructive. If, on the other hand, I feel that my god is the god who has created all things, I move into a world without caring and in the end I am the agent of a mechanistic genius, who performs nothing except with selfish ends. This is the nature of atheism: since there is no personal god, I can easily usurp the creative powers of such a god, and I will certainly be destructive, if you interfere with my particular plan, which I am sure is the right one. We cannot in our present state of culture, which I think will go on indefinitely, pretend that we know the answer to the eternal problems of existence. How can we, when we do not even know how to relate one to another? When we do not know or understand the mystery of life itself, or its deeper nature in death, or how to come to terms with death or what follows death? These are the crucial problems involving all living forms, and we in our own simplicity cannot begin to fathom them with our own native ignorance. When we are still we may begin to learn and to know something of the nature of reality. One thinks of the sentence: 'Be still and know that I am God', in its proper context (Psalm 46.10). We know that we ourselves cannot understand the nature of God or his purpose until we are still and listen, rather than put our own interpretation and wishes first. The more I wish for things, or will things according to my own desire, the more I will begin to hate other people who get in my way, and the more inevitable does war become at one time or another.

All this proves is that human beings are still in a juvenile state of development. We know what we want, but what other people want becomes unimportant if, indeed, not an embarrassment, and we are concerned to move beyond them, so that what we want may be ultimately fulfilled. In the end, their desires have to be completely annulled. When we can face this situation in truth, we can be in charge and know the world, and then our state of anguish can be relieved. Unfortunately, this fulfilment produces anguish in other people, whose view of life is different from ours and whose experience in life has been different as well. None of our experiences are particularly pleasant in the end. I spoke previously about the Job experience, and this is exactly what anybody who is a real person has to undergo. One person has to undergo a destruction of health at an early age, another will lose a close relative or someone they love very deeply. Someone else will find that all their hopes on a personal or material level are dashed in the very process of life, and everything that they had lived for vanishes from their very hands, as it did in the case of Job. Then they have to realize that they have nothing to stand on at all, on a material level; it is only then that the God of true religion can come to their aid.

What is the true God? Can we say that the God of
Christianity is better than the god of the other great religions,
remembering that Buddhism on this level is atheistic and that
it does not believe in a personal god at all? In fact all the
particular views of God are right in their own way, and even
the negativity of atheism is not exactly what it seems. The
Buddhist simply says that god cannot be known and whatever one says about him is untrue and therefore it is better to
be quiet. Once one is sure that one's own view of God is
right, only war can prevail. This is certainly true of theistic
religion – the religion of the Jews, the Muslims, and the
Christians. Hinduism and Buddhism know more about the
power of silence, in which a truer understanding of God may
be given to them. They all know that they of themselves are
nothing at all, but the real God comes to them in their
ignorance and their humility. So if I in my particular religious
frame try to bring virtue in a particular way of life, I am
simply trying to prove to you that my understanding is right
and that your hope of success or life itself depends on your
holding my particular views. This leads inevitably to war and
desolation. That God is not the God of Abraham, Isaac and
Jacob; it is the god of myself. In such a situation I can cause
a tremendous amount of havoc, being the supreme arbiter of
religious orthodoxy and truth.

Therefore nobody can know the fullness of God, whether
the God of theism or the God of one of the great religions of
the East, who are so silent in terms of this great mystery, but
are not ignorant by any means. As we have already said,
Hinduism thinks of God as 'not this, not that', while
Buddhism knows of God as the 'great emptiness (or void)',
but in that emptiness the fullness of reality is contained. It is
not anything in our understanding of the meaning of the
word: nothing is rather the idea of 'no thing'. The Buddhist
understanding of reality is indeed 'no thing': neither this,
that, nor anything else but, rather, a void, as it is sometimes
called, in which everything is contained: you, me, the world,
the universe, it is so vast that it cannot be contained by any
one living concept to the exclusion of any others. If I were to

try to convince you that my understanding of God, according to, say, Christianity, which is my particular faith, was far more accurate than the others, I would simply be trying to convert you to a particular point of view, in the course of which I would prove how little I really knew about the total God of humanity, and of Jesus as well.

Jesus certainly was not dogmatic about the nature of God. Rather, his life revealed God, during which he was not afraid at the end to cry out 'My God, my God, why have you forsaken me?' (Matthew 27.46), a tremendous cry of anguish from one who we Christians believe was God in human form. God could never really forsake one, because the Divine nature is always to have mercy, but in Jesus' state of anguish when he was about to be crucified, he saw that everything that he had stood for in his life had apparently gone up in flames, and that he too, like those before him, was about to be destroyed brutally and cruelly. But he went on in simple faith. In the end he won through, and was able to show the nature of courage and truth in the face of cruelty. It is, indeed, a terrible thought that through the centuries the same religion has been guilty of the destruction of so many people through crucifixions, pogroms and other forms of slaughter, when various groups have tried to prove that they alone have a monopoly on the right doctrine, and they alone know the true God.

If I were to try and prove to you now that I know God, and that only I could give you the truth, I would simply be saying that I am God and you should listen to me and be full of my particular knowledge. It would do you no good at all because I would not be giving you the truth, even if I was absolutely earnest in what I said. God cannot be named, nor can he be described, but he can be known in the soul by the change he produces in all of us and that change is a movement from dogmatic certainty to inward anguish, which ultimately is fulfilled in a new understanding of reality.

I believe the earthly Christ himself had to undergo this particular series of transformations until he knew the resurrection in its completeness.

# 11 Job revisited

We visited Job first in Chapter 2 and considered his initial prosperity and happiness and then his descent into pure hell and how he was salvaged, as it were, from death and destruction by the munificence of God in a magnificent act of grace. But neither he nor we understood the cause of his débâcle. He simply was lucky to be kept alive and, indeed, to be restored to his previous happiness. Now, as we come towards the end of the book, we may perhaps be able to consider the whole question of suffering in relation to Job at a more mature level.

Why did Job have to suffer as he did? The reason was that his way of life was previously inadequate. We came to this conclusion in the second chapter of this book. He depended very much on God to protect him and his family, his money, and his possessions. He was perpetually afraid that some dreadful disaster might overtake them all. And so he sacrificed animals in plenty, and did everything possible to placate God, and do what the law, and particularly his interpretation of the law, required. One does not have to go very far to see how selfish he was in his attitude. How little faith he really had in God, and how desperately he depended on his relationships and his possessions to keep him sound and even sane, and yet he knew intuitively that all this had to go, as it has to go in the case of all of us, as we proceed through life to the inevitable death that terminates all our plans and prosperity and relationships that we may have treasured one with another.

There is one thing that is certain about our lives: it is their transience. None of us is here for any great length of time, as I have already pointed out and, indeed, if this were not the case, the overcrowding in the world would be intolerable. Nobody would have any chance of actualizing their own particular talents or capabilities. All this is perfectly logical, but nobody likes to follow it up in their own particular lives or those of their family. We are always different, as indeed we are of course, but not different in the way of common sense; different rather in the way of being more valuable than other people, and yet we know intuitively how wrong this is.

Through the world's tragedies, in all the centuries, there has been destruction after destruction of human beings. What was hoped for has not come to pass, and people have died. Two chapters from the books of the prophets give us some understanding. From the first of the writing prophets, Amos:

> Spare me the sound of your songs; I cannot endure the music of your lutes. Instead, let justice roll on like a river and righteousness like a never-failing torrent. Did you bring me the sacrifice and gifts, you people of Israel, those forty years when you were in the wilderness? No! But now you shall take up the shrine of your idol king and the pedestals of your images which you have made for yourselves, and I will drive you into the exile beyond Damascus. So says the Lord; the God of Hosts is his name. (Amos 5.23–27)

The other quotation, which we have already considered, comes from Micah.

> What shall I bring when I come before the Lord, when I come to bow before God on High? Am I to approach him with whole offerings, with yearling calves? Will the Lord be pleased with thousands of rams or ten thousand rivers of oil? Shall I offer my eldest son for my wrongdoing, or my child for the sin I have committed? The Lord has told you mortals what is good, and what it is that the Lord asks of you: only to act justly, to love loyalty and to walk wisely before your God. (Micah 6.6–8)

These are the ways that Job learnt through experience. Furthermore, he was deriving something from it. Is it right that we should do well in order to get something out of life, to be more prosperous? Please God, however we may understand God, I think it is very wrong, because that self-centredness makes us alien to our less fortunate fellow creatures so that we at least may succeed, even if they fail. If I was here to show you how successful I was and how much better you would be if you followed me, I would not be doing you any benefit at all, but would rather be irritating you by my complacency and my assurance that I was among the better of the people you knew. And here we come to the root of Job's own inadequacy.

As Blake taught us, pain is the virtuous ego that attributes to itself the virtues of the natural man, as do those social reformers who pride themselves on their concerns for those for whom material good works are so highly regarded if society believes that man may live by bread alone. Blake understood that all these works were unavailing because the selfhood cut off from the living ground of the divine body has no real knowledge of what is good or needful, either for the individual or for mankind as a whole. Blake sought to teach the sons of Eton that however great and glorious, however loving and merciful the individuality, however high our palaces and cities, however fruitful our hills, self would bear nothing but fade away in the morning's breath. Our selfhood is nothing, and love, the great healer and none but the lamb of God, can alone heal the great disease.

Job lived in such a state of mind. Blake used the story of Job as a parable to expose the falsity of natural religion, and of the morality of the self-righteous individuality. This would apply even more today to the permissive society and the trend towards atheism, but was he justified in seeing Job as an exemplar of self-righteousness? Certainly it is a possible reading of the book, and so was understood by St Gregory the Great. It is therefore an orthodox Christian reading, so far as it goes. Blake, of course, carries the attack further by seeing self-righteousness as the inevitable result of materialistic thought and natural religion. But his view of Job is not in this respect unorthodox. There was a difference of opinion about Elihu's criticism of Job, but that criticism in itself was based on Job's self-righteousness. Elihu said in his speech in which he criticizes Job and his three orthodox friends, that Job has consistently insisted on his own righteousness, defending himself and blaming God. Job said, I am righteous and God has taken away my judgement. Elihu had listened carefully to Job's words and his judgement is supported by the text. Job's self-justification has been absolute.

In a passage of great eloquence Job describes himself as he had been in the days when he was universally honoured. 'My righteousness clothed me and my judgement was as a robe and a diadem.' He tells of his many acts of goodness, and as the passage concludes: 'I should plead the whole record of my life and present that in court as my defence.' Elihu became very angry not only because Job had made himself more righteous than God but that his three friends had offered no satisfactory solution. Elihu had his answer, that Job was clearly not in the right, for God is greater than any mortal (Job 33.12). Why then plead your case with him, for nobody can answer his arguments? Indeed, once God has spoken, he does not speak a second time to confirm it. In dreams, in visions of the night, when deepest slumber falls on mortals, while they lie asleep in bed, God imparts his message, and as a warning strikes them with terror. It is clear that Elihu sees in Job the basis of insolent pride, for he has boosted his own previous character and actions, virtually to the level of God himself. This insolent pride is called *hubris*, an overweening pride, leading to its antithesis, which is known as *nemesis*. (Nemesis is the goddess of retributive justice in Greek mythology.) This is where Job went basically wrong.

He was extremely satisfied about his goodness which showed itself in the wonderful prosperity he and his family enjoyed. He almost certainly looked down on other people, although he does not say so directly in the script, but a person who could have said the things that he did say, particularly after his downfall when he was suffering greatly, showed how much he valued his own witness, and how he looked down on those who waited on him carefully to hear what he had to say, until he had nothing more to say at all. So his own *hubris*, or insolent pride, was followed by the *nemesis* of complete destruction. Then he had to face the fact that he as well was nothing in his own right. That is the whole point of Job's story and our own life. We are nothing of our own right at all. Only when we can face this directly and not delude ourselves, can we start to live the proper life. That is ultimately what doubt is about, the doubt which leads to truth. If I have no doubt, if I am sure of my own way and self-importance, if I know that what I do, believe, and say is right, and there is no doubt in my attitude, there is no means of growth or even of communication with other people whom I may regard as grossly inferior to me intellectually, morally, and socially, none of this is of any value at all. If quoting Martin Buber again, all real living is meeting, there is no meeting at all where there is no doubt, because I have the answer and can only repeat it dogmatically to you, but I cannot listen at all to what you have to say to me, particularly in your own suffering and misery.

That is the point of the Job experience, seen not in terms of the horrors that God has visited on a poor, defenceless individual for no apparent rhyme or reason, but to bring him on his way to becoming a full human being able to relate to a host of people whom before he would hardly have noticed as people in their own right.

No, we are nothing in our own right at all, and we only become something when we are nobodies. Then we can relate with other nobodies, and in being a nobody we can become Jesus Christ himself who was merely a carpenter's son when he was alive and died the death of a criminal. We often forget this about our Saviour, who, for this reason alone, in my opinion, surpasses all the other great teachers and masters of the world.

The glory of Jesus does not depend on the brilliance of his resurrection, or any other miraculous event from outside, although I accept them all, and respect them more than I could possibly say. But it is the inner man that makes me sure of his divinity: that he came up from nothing and descended into nothing, but on the third day rose into the fullness of such being that all people were inspired by his example and his growth in their own soul.

As I have said before, the miracle of the physical resurrection, which I accept entirely on intuitive grounds, cannot be proved, except to those who have an inner revelation. But that is not the ultimate way. We do not prove God by miracles. We live by proving God in our own lives, so that we may be sure of God in that he now lives in us. Our God is a living God, and the proof of his life is what he does in us. That is really the basis of theism, and why deism, or natural religion, is a mere travesty of religion.

Deism, or natural religion, is a religion of the mind; it conjures up a god to explain various phenomena. Scientists are particularly effective deists on that level, if indeed they need a god at all. Ultimately such a point of view moves into impersonal atheism, which is probably more honest on an atheistic level than any other. But we who know the truth, know that God lives in us and changes us, as he changed the disciples and Saul, who met the risen Christ. They knew, and we who know God know as well, and enter into a new phase of reality. No longer do we need the sort of proof that a scientist requires in order to believe; we know because we are changed and now can enter into Christhood.

Our life will never be changed until we are all Christs. This does not mean that we all should be replicas of Jesus, but that the spirit which inspired Jesus and is the Holy Spirit which guides all of us and gives us life, being the Lord, the giver of life, makes us full people in our own right. It would be dreadful, indeed, if we were all the same, but the very fact of our individuality means that we all have something unique to give and to show people in our particular way – the fullness of being, as revealed in Jesus. But as I speak to you now, under the guidance of the Holy Spirit, I am one with my Lord, and you are also one, and everyone who listens and has moved beyond mere cerebration is in Christ as well.

This does not mean that we have to forfeit our cerebral

activity and accept spirituality in terms of ignorance. The cerebral mind, the mind of reasoning, is also part of the work of God, but it rises beyond the *hubris*, the insolent pride of human understanding, only when it comes close to ultimate reality. Then we can know the truth which alone can set us free from illusion. The illusion of the human being is that their life is isolated, limited, is alone important, and that they have to live in continual competition with others, and in the end win. But that I should win and prove that I am right and you are wrong is the futility of human existence.

When one knows the truth that sets one free, the idea of personal victory is childish – as childish as winning a game on the sports field. What is important is that we may grow together and change the world, not in the form of a sports field but in the form of a place of universal harmony where we may live and bring joy and happiness to all that lives. It is then that we will know that there is no death; that those who are dead to the body and those who are still alive in the body are indeed one, because we will see ourselves in a completely new framework of reality and then we will know that God is with us as much when the body is dead as when it is alive. As I have already said, death of the body must occur or else the overcrowding of the world would be intolerable, but that is not important. What is important is the animating spirit that brings the body to life, that makes the body useful and of universal relevance and when it has had its day, it goes, and we in our universal spirit go on and produce great things on other levels.

The really great human achievements are not done on a physical level but on the level of the Spirit. The great artists, writers, musicians, and also those involved in scientific and other work are all concerned in changing the world and bringing it intentionally to a better, more fruitful place. This, however, is not inevitable. Our own mind has to play its part as well. I might, for instance, have a very great gift in one particular field, but if I do not use it fruitfully, it will be destructive rather than helpful. We shall consider the ultimate relationship between faith and creativity in the last chapter of this book, but until we have faith, we cannot use our natural gifts properly; we will either try to prove that we are better than other people or else try to benefit ourselves on a personal level, or in some way be destructive; we will never grow up, in other words. The faith of God helps us grow up from immaturity to maturity, and from maturity to immortality.

Human beings are naturally immortal, as indeed I believe all creation is, but that immortality is irrelevant until we can use it. What is the use of my going on in the living form, however we may envisage this? It would obviously be a psychic form rather than a purely physical one. If I cannot give any help to others to grow into their fullness of being as well, I am a mere nothing, but once I can give, and change the world through my influence and what I am inwardly, then I become a saint in my own life: a follower and manifestation in my own way of the Lord Jesus, in whom the Spirit works perfectly and through whom I may know the Spirit, and from whom I may reveal the Father to all people.

We grow into the knowledge of God primarily through our experience of Jesus, who leads us to the work of the Holy Spirit, and in the Holy Spirit, the Lord and giver of life, we see the ultimate Lord and giver of all life, who is God the Father. God the Father comes to us through the Son and the Holy Spirit. I am not for one moment saying that one is more important than the other, but I am giving an order of primacy. We know the Son, who is human as we are, and therefore is closest to us in divine relationship, but in that relationship we know something that we would not have known otherwise, the Holy Spirit, who brings us to full life, the life that was shown definitively in the life of Jesus, and in the combination of the Son and Spirit we know the one from whom both emanate and grow, namely the Father.

This is why in the end the trinitarian scheme of reality is the most satisfactory. I am not here trying to be polemical, or prove that one religion is better than the other, but if we do understand the meaning of the Holy Trinity, we can understand the significance of God's nature to us in eternity, in a way that can bring our life into permanent relevance. So it is really the Son, Holy Spirit and Father. We know the Father last of all because he is greatest of all. First, the Son is closest to us in being, then the Spirit who flows or proceeds from the Son and then the Father, by whom we know both the Spirit and the Son, and we see that the Father shows us the way that the Son works; the Son is, indeed, the image of the eternal Father. Not one is greater than the other, all three are part of an amazing synthesis of reality, and once you know one permanently and definitively, then you know the others as well and you come closer and closer to ultimate reality.

That is the way in which we know Job as well. Nobody here has ever met him, but we understand his nature much as we do when we believe we are strong. But in our weakness the Spirit can flow through us and he begins to show us the truth. And following truth we begin to understand. So also Job, once he has seen the fullness of God in the divine epiphany, says

> I know that you can do all things and that no purpose is beyond
> you. But I have spoken of things that I have not understood;
> things too wonderful for me to know. I knew you then only by
> report, but now I see you with my own eyes. Therefore I yield,
> repenting in dust and ashes. (Job 42.1–6)

That is the whole point. Of course, Job cannot see God, but he sees the nature of God and he understands the meaning of God's works as well. Nothing is hidden from Job now that he is far from self-regard, as well as any intolerable suffering. He knows that he knows nothing and that he is in a state of divine knowledge. He who believes that he knows, knows nothing. He who knows that he knows nothing is coming towards understanding. One will never attain that full understanding but at last one is beginning to know the truth. So Job's suffering has brought him to the truth, the truth that he is an impotent, unimportant individual with a certain amount of money, children and power, but is groping towards death as we all do.

But then in his suffering he begins to know the meaning of nobility as well, that although we are all dust, ashes, worms or whatever analogy with which you like to compare humans, when they face the inevitable in calm strength and restraint, they enter into something of the nature of a real human being, and in this respect Job and Jesus have more than a little in common – except that Jesus faced his end with a complete quietness from the beginning to the ultimate destruction, whereas Job could only fight and try to justify himself, since he realised that self-justification was completely irrelevant.

Who cares about what Job did, or what people thought about him in the olden days? It is simply past history now. It is what he is now, and what he shows himself to be now in his desolation, that makes him important. And that applies to all of us as well. When things go well with us, we tend to have too high an opinion of ourselves, thinking that people ought to honour us because of our success, but when we have failed, or what we regard as failure, and still go on day by day, then we begin to know the meaning of real success, in the world's understanding of that word. But unfortunately, this type of success is not popular in the usual secular type of society.

I spoke about the Job experience, how I myself have had to go through it in a state of complete weakness and pain in my limbs in such a way that I can hardly do anything for myself. And at that time I was very sorry for myself, even weeping for a time. Now I am no longer in a weeping mood. I am only grateful to God for showing me so many things that I would not have understood otherwise. While in no way ashamed of my emotional outpouring, it is always good to be honest with other people about how one feels and not put on the 'stiff upper lip'.

I am even more grateful now to be able to face whatever is in front of me, whether death, permanent crippledom, or at least some degree of impairment of movement again. It does not matter in the end. This is the important thing. What is important is that my life, or Job's, or Jesus', or anybody else's, should be of value to other people, not merely by example, but by giving something of themselves as well. Jesus gave everything of himself.

Job learned to give much of himself, which did not depend on material possessions, and I, in an infinitely lesser way than either of these two great ones, have still been able to give something of myself through my own particular mental abilities. This is the joy of living – being able to enrich those who do not understand life through one's own experience. One cannot understand except through experience. Let us follow that and accept it right away. You do not understand truth by reading books, but by going through an experience with vitality, strength, and complete honesty. Then the truth will be revealed to you, but if you try to avoid it, or make a bargain with God, your bargain will be ignored before it is even registered. But when we are strong in our own resolve, we will never be far from our Creator, and then we will know God.

That is ultimately in fact the meaning of Job's story. It is far more important than any other explanation that I have given in this book. Once we are full human beings, we can give of our fullness to those around us, whether they are male or female, young or old, rich or poor; we are all of these things, in fact, if we knew ourselves properly, and we should not judge according to such differentiations. Then we would know that we are creatures of God, suffering in our own weakness, and yet also part of the full Christ who is the total humanity. Remember that this is really what Christ is about; not a single remarkable human being, but the fullness of humanity, made obvious to us, as each performs their particular work in the world, so they become full of their own being, and do the work as is set before them likewise.

It is good in a way to be sorry for oneself. I have no objection to that, for it is human and honest. So therefore the performance that I put on in Chapter 6 does not in any way embarrass me, but it would be a great shame if even now I performed in the same manner. It would simply have meant that I had not learned and that I was still hankering after past ways and not getting on with my life, a life which is not to be lived in order to show how capable I am, but in order to give to other people something of the manifold mental and spiritual gifts that fall from me as from a fountain. You do not have to be especially spiritually aware to see that it does flow from me on that level, just as you would not need to have very great depth to see into my character.

'Strength is made perfect in weakness. My grace is all you need', St Paul tells us in 2 Corinthians 12.9. That is really what inspiration is about. Whether one is weak in one part of the body or other, if we are in Christ and believing in God, strength comes to us and what appears to be a curse becomes a blessing. We can then do, understand, or say things that we could never have done, said, or understood before, and then whatever we do becomes a blessing to so many people. If I was an ordinary man I would behave in an ordinary way, looking for what I could get out of life, women, money, social importance, and other worldly things.

There is nothing wrong in this; please do not accuse me of sneering at it, why should not I also have as much money as possible, enjoy an active sex life, and know many important people? But a surfeit does become rather futile in the end. On the other hand, if one is open to the power of God and can understand spiritual things, not only speaking about them but also knowing about them and showing them to others, their lives can be transformed. And then a new world can come into being. That is exactly what happened through Jesus and the various disciples and apostles who followed him. Through him a new creation was indeed set up and its end is still far from over, although many people have done their best to destroy it in one way or another.

There is one other thing I ought to admit before I leave this chapter: my rather critical view of liberal religion, natural religion, and deism. After all, God is mentioned there as well, but it is seldom a living God. It is, rather, a god that is involved with the formation or creation of the human mind. It is an explanation for the various phenomena of the universe. It plays a part in Unitarianism and Quakerism as well. This is why these two religions are not particularly popular at the present time. This applies particularly to the Unitarian form. Quakers will always have their own significance because of their spirituality and their way of worship. But you cannot easily worship a god in a deistic form. Why should there be a god who creates in the first place? His only reason for creating is surely love, in other words, the god that is the true God is a living god and his life is shown not in the fact that he creates, but that he loves his creation which he fills with his own love, so that it may reflect his love.

It is for this reason that what is called liberal religion is not particularly popular at the moment. I certainly would not strive to convert people away from it, any more than I would want to convert them to strongly fundamentalist types of Catholicism or Evangelicalism. They all have their strength undoubtedly, but their weakness is not hidden from any eye either. The last two are grossly intolerant, this is really their trouble, particularly when they believe that they have the full answer to life. Some Unitarianism and Quakerism has more or less moved away from the living God altogether into a type of god that satisfies the mind or intellect without inducing much compassion.

As in everything else in the world, these statements need qualification: there are wonderful Protestants and Catholics whose lives are devoted to the benefit of their fellow creatures. On the other hand, there are especially highly charismatic forms of these religions which can be very dangerous because of their dogmatism associated with strongly superstitious trends. Whenever superstition comes in, fear and hatred follow. The results are not good, since they also diminish the integrity of the human mind.

Whenever you start to get involved in religion, as Job did, you are exposed to all sorts of dangers, from psychical to intellectual states of being. I have already discussed the psychical aspect of religion and shown how dangerous it can be, but I would still rather have the danger of religion, even in its most unpleasant forms, than a type of dull, uniform agnosticism which does not really accept anything at all, apart from the immediate evidence of the senses. This type of religion is hardly human. It may be safe, but it leads nowhere in particular, and in the end, you are, like Job, fearing for the thing that was to come to you (Job 3.25).

# 12 Equanimity and integrity

'He who doubts from what he sees, will ne'er believe, do what you please' (*Auguries of Innocence* by William Blake). That is the basis of doubt in its most negative form. Such a person will never, ever accept anything except on a very personal level and that you cannot find absolutely in this life. Ultimately you have to go via a considerable number of criteria, just as when you read this now you have to feel your way to my thought by understanding me and seeing what you can see, and also seeing what you do not want to see, because I am not the arbiter of ultimate truth.

I would first of all like to consider the meaning of equanimity. One of the antidotes to destructive doubt is equanimity, which means evenness of mind or temper, composure and resignation. There are many things in life which we do not understand, and the more we try and penetrate their mystery through the intellect, the more confused and unhappy we become. Eventually we have to understand that there is no intellectual answer to our problems; and I am speaking here on a very personal level: 'Why does this have to happen to me and my family?' These are the sorts of questions that I was pondering on in the second chapter of this book. In the end, there is no answer to these problems at all that will give us that degree of security or peace of mind that we all long for, and which, if we actually shared, might cause us paradoxically to become increasingly depressing and frustrating to other people.

When one knows equanimity, there is an evenness of mind and temper, so that whatever happens we are in the hands of a providence far higher than we are, which can show us the way forward. Composure and its rather more negative form resignation again help us onwards. When I can be composed, sure of my own being and strength, even when the most unpleasant things are happening to me, I am of most use to humanity. It is lack of composure that characterized Job when he was groaning, comparing his exalted state in the past with his negative state in the present. Had he known composure, he would never have spoken in that negative way at all.

How can you become composed? You can certainly become composed by being more open to yourself and seeing all life as a journey towards death and destruction. That is a negative way of composure, by no means to be dismissed out of hand, but it does not lead you very far in the end; it suggests that criminal and saint alike go to the same place. They share the same fate, and whatever they do, is fulfilled in same state of futility. There is a great deal of truth in what I have said, and yet this is also far from satisfactory as witnessed in the difference between the way of the saint and that of the sinner. If you are saintly, you foster love in other people, and form the focus of a new community, whereas if you are the conventional sinner you are interested in selfish pursuits, have no real friends, and when you move towards the inevitable state of death, nobody mourns your passing very much.

The word 'parasite' can justifiably be used in the case of the most perpetual sinner. It is not a very pleasant word, but one I know very well from my relationships with a certain type of person. In my work as one who tries to help people on the spiritual path, there are many who do not really listen at all, their souls seem to be closed, and when they depart, they are manifestly as unchanged as when they arrived. I have learnt that these people are perpetual drainers, perpetual parasites on the psychical level, and eventually if they are not confronted with their own uselessness, they can cause a great deal of psychical damage, and eventually indeed one may have to cease seeing them, at least temporarily, until they come to their senses. Their strong point of contact is with the physical (bodily) and psychical (emotional) parts of the personality.

You can never impose equanimity on people. There will always be the type of person who says 'Why did this have to happen to me, I didn't deserve it?' and it goes on for a little while, as Job himself did after a short time. Composure and particularly equanimity do not ask these questions. They strive to fend them off and use them constructively. If I know equanimity in its fullness of being, my mind and temper are balanced; they are in a state of equality and I do not expect anything as my due. That is where we go wrong in our lives, expecting benefits of one type or another, as if we ourselves were particularly deserving in acquiring them.

In our lives we are not in a position to expect anything at all, except the three ultimate prerogatives, ageing, disease and death, which the Buddha enumerated some thousands of years ago. But if we expect benefits of one type of another, we are bound to be disappointed, because we are not living the right life. Even if I now were expecting you to think well of me, have a high opinion of me, and regard me as something of a spiritual authority, I would soon get in the way and my equanimity would fail immediately. I would assume an air of learning and graciousness, so that you might be impressed and consider me a person of great gifts, whereas in fact I am the most ordinary of people, sometimes below ordinary as well, I might add.

When you know equanimity you do not expect anything at all, you are only grateful for what you have been given through the grace of God, and do not expect extra gifts above what you already have. The great gift that we all share is this gift of grace: unmerited holiness from God which we are expected to use for our own benefit and the benefit of others. It comes to us from on high. We cannot even begin to understand it properly. It is the gift that is in store for all of us who are able to receive it. You do not receive grace because you earn it or deserve it, you receive it because God loves you, but you in return have to accept that love and to be its transmitter to the whole world, otherwise the grace ceases to flow through you and you become a dead object. St Paul says in the famous 1 Corinthians 13:1-3:

> I may speak in tongues of men and of angels but if I am without love I am a sounding gong or a clanging cymbal. I may have the gift of prophecy and know all living truth, I may have faith strong enough to move mountains, but if I have no love I have nothing. I may dole out all I possess and even give my body to be burned, but if I have no love, I am none the better.

This is the whole point of the matter. In a state of equanimity you can give out that love without expecting anything in return, not because nothing has previously been given to you, but because now your ego and your feelings of dereliction and disappointment, and all the other egoistical views of life, are simply overwhelmed by the love of God. Then there is peace in your mind and a feeling of great harmony and goodness – at last you can be free from all expectation of things to come in the future.

Job was a happy man as far as anyone could be happy. There was a feeling of basic insecurity, however. Nevertheless, he did all the things that should have been done at that time: making many sacrifices, being a good father, and probably husband as well as far as we can tell; his behaviour was immaculate, and yet he got no benefit from it at all. Instead a great tragedy afflicted him. It did not make sense at all, and he could not understand why. 'If only someone could show me why, what I had done wrong' and his comforters showed him that he was a miserable sinner and that he did not have the proper faith to continue. He was, in fact, a sinner, though not of the type the comforters would have understood. He put himself and his family first; that was the whole trouble about Job, when one considers his predicament in a more personalistic form.

When he goes on to justify himself, in that passage from Job 29 – 31 that I have already quoted on two occasions, he describes his happiness in the past and how everybody in the community looked up to him as a man of holiness and wisdom. And now he is no better than a slave. But how he did love himself before! How *hubris*, self-opinionation, did govern his life! And now it had been taken away from him in one fell swoop and he was nothing at all. That was a tragic situation for a person who had identified himself with his works. Works that come not through God but from the human being, so as to show how excellent one is and how far better one is than one's fellow creatures, are soon fraught with a relapse of illness.

This, as I said before, is the reason why the welfare-state type of approach to health and humanity, though so excellent on the surface, is so inadequate on a deeper level: because it does not work towards the change of people. It is good that people may be better in health, but it is only important if that health is a manifestation of inner sanctity, otherwise one type of ill-health will be followed quite certainly by another, and in the end the person will not have benefited greatly.

When one knows equanimity, one knows inner peace and strength, and then one does not need to expect anything any more, or look for anything, or want anything as a sort of reward for one's actions. One realizes that the state of inner peace and sanctity is the reward. That is how we always know God, not by outer manifestations but by the inner change that occurs within us, so that at last we can say 'I see with my own eyes' as Job did. Not with the outer eyes, quite obviously, but with the inner eye of deep faith. It is not faith in believing something; it is faith in knowing something on the deepest level.

This is the ultimate faith, and then you can begin to see the meaning of Job's suffering and the meaning of his coming through it as well. His vision at the beginning was clouded, largely with his personality and selfishness, but in the end there was nothing left for him to cling on to at all, and then in that state of complete emptiness, he knew the one thing that was needful was salvation, namely God himself, who is known to the mystic as 'The Supreme Emptiness', and 'the Cloud of Unknowing'. We have mentioned this already in previous chapters. No one has ever seen God or ever could see God on a personal level. Such a god would undoubtedly be an illusion or a fraud.

It is God who opens our spiritual eyes, so that we can see clearly, perhaps for the first time in our lives, who brings us towards the truth, which is fully of a divine nature. That is how God shows himself to us, so that we can see clearly the things of eternity and work towards them, by bringing that knowledge closer to other people. We do this not by teaching or by speaking about it to them, but by showing it to them in our own lives. Even in my completely inadequate presentation here, if I have helped to clear your eyes of various illusions, so that you might see literally nothing at all, you would still be very near to God, because in that nothing, everything is contained, and the love of God is the basis of every word, every action that I make. I obviously could not claim such a glory for myself, but I know what it is about.

If you are with people who have that great love, you will know that in them God resides in a very perfect way and through them you will know God, perhaps for the first time in your life. It is not whether they want money or power, but what they want in themselves. In equanimity you really want nothing at all; first, because you have it all already, and, second, because you want to give your blessings to other people. Then the whole world may be filled with equanimity.

People may be full of their own glory in the knowledge of God. If I am a person of glory it is because I am close to my Maker, not because I have done anything at all, even if indeed I had great talents of one type or another, they would be sure to be superseded by other people with greater talents in due course, probably very soon. But if I am still in the presence of God, what I have said can never be superseded, because it is of the nature of reality, and in this way I can show you how through the basis of equanimity you too can share with me the eternal mystery of God, which is closer to us than our own heartbeat – because it is absolutely love.

And now let us think about integrity. Integrity may be defined as soundness, uprightness, and honesty. It is in its own way the other part of equanimity. With its soundness, uprightness, and honesty it seeks for nothing that is not itself. It is close indeed to the nature of God. A person of integrity is upright and honest; there is soundness and complete truth in their behaviour. One can trust that person absolutely because they do not depend on their own reputation any more, nor do they desire any of the things of this world. Everything of this world that person may have is blessed because they are close to God, and in God a new creation is born. The soundness and wholeness bring them absolutely close to the formative elements of all being. And now there is equanimity as well. The lack of demands that a person of equanimity has, so that the present moment is good enough for them, extends also to a person of integrity. One can trust them absolutely because they have no ulterior motives. All they want is to do the work of God and bring that work into the world. This is done in the spirit of equanimity, or complete availability to God at any moment, no longer seeking for oneself, or worrying about what has been done, or should be done, or has not been done, but giving of oneself absolutely, in the spirit of prayer and thanksgiving.

When you know integrity, you know complete freedom of the spirit because now no one can touch you any more. They may attack you, you may be the victim of scandal and cruelties of various types, and yet it does not matter because you know that all this is clearly malicious. There have been martyrs of persecution throughout all the centuries, but their martyrdom has been ultimately a mark of respect because they have shown an equanimity in a spirit of complete self-giving, whereby they may know the power of God as he works in their own lives.

A person of integrity is one who is absolutely secure in their relationships with others, who makes no demands on anyone else, and is absolutely clear in what they need and do not need, and does not in any way force themself on others. Their work is entirely to bring the presence of God to others, that they too may live a life of integrity and bring that wholeness to the whole world.

Needless to say, integrity is not a common state amongst

humans, who are seduced by the things of this world, almost to the complete exclusion of anything else. But if you know integrity, you know the nature of God. God does not make demands. He does not tell you what you should do and what you should not do. He certainly is no hard task-master. He is there to prove to you that by being what you are made of and what you are fit to do you may become a real person in your own right. In your reality, you are able to give of yourself fully to others as well.

If in equanimity you can take life as it comes moment by moment, and in integrity you can follow through and give of that life to others moment by moment, so equanimity becomes an apt precursor of integrity. The person of equanimity gives moment by moment in order that, through their dedication that may go to the person with integrity, they may proceed and receive more and more from the person of equanimity.

These two gifts of the spirit, equanimity and integrity, are the most beautiful that God has shown us. Both are manifested in the life of Jesus. Think of Jesus' life, for instance. In the early stages he was a highly charismatic leader. Nearly all he said was misconstrued by his contemporaries, but he was able to escape from a dilemma every time when it was necessary. But in the end he fell victim to the forces of evil who planned his crucifixion. He did not turn a hair, as we might say, but saw what was to happen to him and did not plead in any way with Pilate, or anyone else to save himself or get him out of his predicament. He was in a state of quiet trust even as the crucifixion proceeded, before the miraculous resurrection restored the faith of the apostles. There was never any evidence of fear of any type, yet I am sure that he suffered greatly, for I do not see him as a superman who was beyond all these things.

His suffering was quite as great as any of our sufferings would be in a similar situation, but there was somehow an equanimity about his approach which took it in his stride, so that when the time came for him to die, he could say 'Father, into your hands I commit my spirit' (Luke 23.46). There was no feeling of anger towards those who had engineered his death, and no fear of what was to come to him either. Of course, on one level, there should have been no fear because his life had been immaculately pure. But be that as it may, as it were, there was still enough fear in terms of physical pain to cause any of us to wince when we think of what he must have gone through. That aspect of death is not removed, no matter how good you might have been.

Some of the most virtuous people I know have suffered abominably before they have died. Now, with powerful anaesthetics and analgesic drugs, the height of pain can be relieved, but this is not really the point at all. The real relief of pain comes from a different attitude of mind to the suffering of the body, rather than taking some medicament which may make us feel better or more composed or more able to compensate for the problems that are to come to us. It is only when we can be fully ourselves in our own being that we know what Jesus actually underwent.

Therefore his integrity was based on equanimity related to a state of mind in which he could follow through that which he was undergoing at the present moment and accept without either reproach or fear or any other negative feeling.

I always stress the fact that Jesus' sufferings were very similar to our own, at least on the bodily level, because he was the Word made flesh and it would have been wrong had he escaped the pain you and I also have to suffer as we grow older and have to face the inadequacies of the body. But he knew what it was about and he showed it by his faith and love to all his human brethren, bringing them up to a higher level of reality.

Think of the disciples and apostles who died more or less at the same time as he did. What an influence he must have had in raising them to the faith that they were also to show! His equanimity also brought him to a state of careless rapture. He did not need to blame anyone for their betrayal. There was no feeling of indignation, or cynicism or disappointment in humanity in general, or his disciples more particularly. How easy it would have been for him to have been angry with his disciples, who had exhibited themselves so badly, despite his presence among them for the three years before his death. But instead he forgave them: 'Father, forgive them, for they know not what they do' (Luke 23.34) is a characteristic saying of Jesus at this time. Forgiveness is always a sign of equanimity.

People are weak. 'The spirit is willing, but the body is weak' (Matthew 26.41) is the way Jesus expressed it. But it is inevitable that, since the body is a pain-bearing organ, if it is hurt it complains in no uncertain way. If you were stabbed, or in some other way beaten up, and you did not show any reaction or pain at all, I would not be impressed. I would suspect rather that there was something wrong with your body, and that you could not react properly. We feel both with our bodies and our emotions, and if either of these is dulled we do not respond properly, there is something wrong with us, and we certainly are not to be envied in our negative reaction.

Jesus had a highly sensitive body and emotional life. He had to be like this, because of the special work that he had to do. So when he experienced the agony in the garden of Gethsemane, and particularly on the cross, he went through it in perfection of emotion, blaming neither the Father nor his disciples, nor Pilate nor any of the members of the Sanhedrin. He went through the whole of the process untouched inwardly. He understood equanimity, and his integrity was such that he never proceeded to blame other people or prove that he really had not said what was alleged, but that other people had misconstrued his teaching; and if only they really understood what he had meant, they would never have put that particular emphasis on his statements. He went by the essence of what he said.

There was nothing that he said on which he ultimately tried to reproach himself. He claimed to have a divine connection, particularly in John's Gospel, and also to a certain extent in the other three as well, and he never denied that ultimate connection before his death. This did not make his ministry any easier; it would have been far better for him had he been just an ordinary human being, very gifted, but still frail and insignificant. But he claimed to be God in the flesh and he proved it as well, not only by the performing of miracles that opened people's eyes, but much more significantly by showing them what a person could do under the influence of the Divine Spirit.

If Jesus had done miracles which manifested his great superiority over other human beings, far from lauding him, I would have been sceptical and a little angry as well. The sort of Christ who is far above me and can bear pain that I cannot bear, is remarkably unhelpful to me, but the type of Christ who can bear exactly what I have to bear in my life, and can bear it in absolute purity of heart and sanctity of spirit, is the type of Christ whom I can worship, follow and bow down before. This is the Christ who is of the nature of God, and we can see what he wants every time he speaks about it. This is a hard saying, of course, for it would be far more agreeable if we all could be delivered time and time again from pain, but we cannot, and we have to grow by faith as well as by love.

Faith comes by following the work of the Holy Spirit, as we are led into new ways of thought and action. The research scientist, the doctor, or anyone who is involved in explorations into new aspects of reality, is involved in the work of the Holy Spirit. There should be no ultimate distinction between the work of the Spirit and the work of the research mind. It is how you use it that matters. A person who has a genius or gift for research work is doing their work properly, and while they are doing it, they may suddenly begin to understand new things which may have an enormous relevance to any number of chronic diseases.

There is no point in any of us being permanently ill or in chronic pain. No good comes out of that. I have never believed that myself; my medical studies and my own personal problems have shown me that this is not the way. If you are alive, you can do much more good if you are healthy in body, mind, soul, and spirit than if any part of your anatomy is out of joint. The value of pain and suffering is that it gets people to empathize better, for at least a time. That time should not go on indefinitely, but be shortened by new findings in anatomy, physiology, pathology and various diseases of the mind, so that the body may now function as a healthy, composite unit. In this way there may be a reunion of body, mind, soul, and spirit, and a more competent integrated person may emerge.

# 13 Doubt and faith

To many people, the antithesis of doubt is faith. If you are a person of faith you do not doubt anything at all, and indeed you would feel somewhat guilty if you doubted any of the divine mysteries of life. Could you doubt God, for instance, or the onward flow of life, whether or not there was survival of physical death? Yet, on the other hand, until you can face these things definitively you cannot be a really honest individual.

Tennyson said:

There lives more faith in honest doubt,
believe me, than in half the creeds.
(*In Memoriam*, XCVI)

We spoke about faith without doubt being dead faith in a previous chapter. What did Tennyson mean when he said that there lives more faith in honest doubt than in half the creeds? In honest doubt you are expressing your own opinion and thinking clearly into the nature of reality. The trouble about credal religion is that one quotes something which eventually becomes almost a word for word quote without thinking very much about what one says. That is one of the reasons why I sympathize with such a religion as Quakerism or Unitarianism that has no formal creed at all – not because I think that creeds are wrong, but because they can often lead one on to smug reassurance. They are all a form of words, as St Paul would have put it (2 Timothy 1.13), they sound good if you really do believe them, and it would be good as well, but as you almost certainly do not understand exactly what you are saying, you begin to delude yourself.

That is why Tennyson's statement that there lives more faith in honest doubt than in reciting half the creeds has a very relevant truth in our lives, particularly today when people will not take statements on trust, simply because they come from a holy, a reliable or even, God forgive me, a scientific source. All these sources are human and therefore liable to error: sometimes terrible error that kills people.

Creeds, on the other hand, are very useful in leading us in the right way to honest doubt, and also to honest education. If you do not claim to accept the trinitarian scheme, and if you aspire to be a Christian, you will not eventually understand what Christianity is about. It is not about believing in the Father, the Son, and the Holy Spirit. It is about living life – a life that comes to terms fully with reality, in the power of the risen Christ, the Father, and the Holy Spirit. Then you have something real to hold on to and something that is meaningful to you. But merely repeating words that sound good to the ear can be a way of escaping reality and your own particular version of truth.

In another well-known poem Emerson writes:

I am the doubter and the doubt,
I am the hymn the Brahmin sings.

It comes from a poem called *Brahma*. Here we have the idea that God is in all things; nothing can be separated from God fully. I am in God, and so are you, and so are the most evil and wicked people. He has created us all; through him we are what we are, and we have to make the best of what we are, often frightful specimens of humanity.

Why are some people born with hereditary diseases of one type or another – epilepsy, or haemophilia, or some diseases of the bones and joints? They did not ask for it, it came to them. It could be said that they inherited it from their parents, but why did their parents have it, and why did they have to inherit it? Most hereditary diseases do not fall on all the offspring of the parents, in any case; some children seem to escape scot-free, while others certainly do not. Why is there this indiscriminate suffering of some, whereas others seem to be completely healthy? This is the sort of question which is at the very basis of doubt. One person suffers the full gamut of tragedy, whereas a close relative comes through and lives a life of ease, good mental activity, and prosperity. Why is there this variation in the person's way of life?

We cannot answer this question on a purely academic level. Ultimately what we have to do is to see what we can make out of our individual life. If I am born a haemophiliac or an epileptic, or someone who suffers from a severe disease of the bones and joints, I am left with it. I can revolt against it, and be extremely angry, and even curse God if I really want to, but it does not help me. God does not mind being cursed. He can carry on very well, but I simply show my anger in a very childish way, and I still have to carry on with the burden which has been placed upon me.

Here we come to something of the solution to the problem. If I can share the problem, I become a greater person, and I begin to understand something about the nature of life and come to terms with other people and their problems in a way that I probably could not do had I been born to health and riches, but unable to empathize with many unfortunate people. Through my own pain, misery, ineptitude, suffering, impotence and all the other negative qualities I can mention, I can come to terms with the suffering of humanity and, indeed, all life. And if I can continue in strength and not revolt against it and be as miserable as possible, I can begin to grow into a real person, something of the nature of the crucified Christ.

Our life on earth is not merely a physical one of being as strong and rich as possible, while enjoying all the good things of the world with all the bodily strength at our disposal. It is here to come to support other people as well and to enrich the whole of creation, the whole created universe. Then we begin to see the meaning of our life here. If we are here simply to be as happy, prosperous, rich, or influential as possible, each of these qualities detracts from this great armamentarium of universal assets and soon we are low, and we depend on the help of other people. That, of course, is no bad thing, for it may make us realize how impotent we are unless we do rely on others, and should not always become absolutely self-sufficient in our own right.

But the very young person could not possibly reach that degree of understanding; they would necessarily compare themself with their contemporaries and prove that they were at least not inferior to them and, indeed, probably superior, because they could run, walk, or do something else better than the other person. When we are young, indeed, we enjoy flourishing and showing ourselves in our own glory. When we get older. it is still satisfying to be able to perform particularly on an artistic level, and we can enjoy new forms of art and see the old fusing with the new, and something of real value coming, but now we can help as much by our teaching ability as by our performance.

Therefore, God is in the doubter and the doubt and in the hymn that the Brahmin sings. He is in everything and the doubter is not greater than the doubt or the spiritual attitude of the Brahmin, the high-caste Hindu priest. He is in all and shows himself in all. What does the hymn that the Brahmin sings have in common with doubt or the doubter? What is common to the three is the fact that the Divine essence inspires them all. The hymn, the doubt, and the doubter are all expressing aspects of ignorance. When one moves beyond them, one is no longer trapped in material thoughts or questions, and can enter a new realm of spirituality. And then we can start to be ourselves.

I can only be myself when I stop asking questions about why I am this, that, or the other, and can instead be fully aware of myself as I am, and give as I am now; and as I give, so will I grow and see things about myself and about the world in which I live and the world beyond which I live. I now know the problem of life generally. In such a situation I can move towards sanctity. This sanctity was shown fully in the lives of the great saints, especially our Lord Jesus Christ. His life never amounted to much in the world's eyes. Now he is the supreme manifestation of the Creator in his fullness of being.

> He who doubts from what he sees,
> will ne'er believe, do what you please.

> If the sun and moon should doubt,
> they'd immediately go out.

> To be in a passion you good may do,
> but no good if a passion is in you.

I have quoted some of these lines from William Blake in a previous chapter. Again, if you doubt on a negative level, you can never proceed. You see more and more of less and less of things. The moon and sun dare not doubt of their particular abilities, because if they do they immediately go out. If you are in a passion, you may do good, but if the passion is in you, you flare up and what is in you extinguishes all that is creative and good and you become a lifeless being; fortunately, this is usually only temporary.

Therefore doubting is of the basis of life. Without it one cannot be a full human being. One is shutting one's eyes to the reality of existence, and in so doing one is shutting one's eyes to the reality of much of human nature, which means in essence one's own nature.

But is there any place for faith if doubt is of the nature of ultimate reality, and all our lives are extinguished in an immediate wind of doubt? Nothing is created that is not worthwhile, but there is surely more to the matter than this. Faith causes us to flourish, and brings out in us a core of positive being. A good example is seen in medical practice, for instance. Take a condition like cancer, which is virtually incurable, particularly in its later, more widespread forms. But more and more has been known about it through constructive therapeutic research, first of all cutting out as much as possible (surgery), and more recently using radiotherapy to destroy as much as possible, with the use of cytotoxic drugs (called chemotherapy), and there are also hormonal and other methods of treatment. They all help us to deal with it.

The condition is still incurable unless it is removed at an early stage of its development, whether by radiotherapy, drugs, or some other means of treatment. But more and more hope has come to us over the years, and now we can face the fact of cancer with greater confidence than in the past. This is the foundation of faith. Many types of cancer spread so rapidly, they are so malignant, as we would say, that they kill in a matter of weeks, or perhaps a few months. These have not been rendered substantially less lethal by any known method of treatment. Others, on the other hand, have been ameliorated considerably, and patients have been known to survive and live much more constructive, prolonged lives than before. That is where faith has modified present doubt, and made cancer far less menacing.

We are not expected to live in doubt; in fact, we are expected to live in knowledge. Knowledge is the full aspect of our existence. But we will never have that full knowledge that is our due, because we are not in a state of understanding to accommodate it. But if we were to know about the nature of the soul after death, we would be in such a state of spiritual understanding that we could grow from the purely physical to the psychical and then to the spiritual mode of existence.

I think the same would apply to a lethal disease like cancer. When we are in a state of grace, when God flourishes in us, we are all inspired by the Holy Spirit, I believe again that so-called spontaneous cures would occur much more frequently and rapidly. What is a miracle at the moment would become very much more frequent; a miracle in this respect being defined as something which makes one wonder because of its marvel. Many of these words simply describe things that we do not understand, but a miracle is something that makes us wonder. The greatest miracle, of course, is life itself: that we survive, that we live in a hostile environment amongst people who do not understand us or life for that matter. Yet we fend for ourselves and grow for ourselves, and survive in a society which is not particularly conducive to personal understanding. We survive, we marry, we procreate, and our children survive as well. It is amazing that in our world that has been so contaminated by warfare at one time or another, especially in our own generation, children have done so well. The promise of the future is good rather than bad, unless humans behave so stupidly that they destroy each other *en masse.*

Life is conducive to faith not doubt. If we live with reasonable common sense the species will survive – indeed, will multiply if we live in complete ignorance concerning contraception, for then human procreation will outrun food supplies and living space. Then alone there is a danger that we will start to fight amongst ourselves and wars of immense destructiveness may develop. Nowadays, responsible people do not go in for warfare. Nothing is ever gained in the long run by trying to get something from another country, by wresting something from it. It is noteworthy that some of the worst-governed countries of the Middle East are the ones that participate particularly in warfare. If only they would govern themselves properly, they would be far happier than by causing a great deal of trouble and misery to those outside themselves!

That is the whole point of the matter. If we are not happy in ourselves, we start doing things that are immoral and destructive. At the end of the day we are thoroughly miserable. Real happiness comes from within when we know the power of the Spirit of God governing our lives and the lives of those around us. When we are not happy we look around us and seek for things that are not really ours at all, and strive for them as our possessions (Matthew 5.23–26). I am not saying from this that the problems of the world are entirely due to hostile attitudes of certain nations in, for instance, the Middle East. I think that would be an over-simplification of a difficult political issue, for even if justice were done according to what these people want, they would still remain unhappy because they would still not be fulfilled as individuals. If I feel that I have been hard done by, that the world has treated me badly, I may behave more and more boorishly and miserably, and I will not really become happy even if what I believe is justice is done, and I will simply look for something else to cast my eyes on and desire. Happiness does not come from possessions: it comes from equanimity.

What then should a nation do that feels it has been hard done by through the perfidy of its neighbours? The answer is quite obvious from the last chapter on equanimity. It should be quiet, still, and worship God, and be open to the divine essence. Then peace will come to it, and it would start to be peaceful to those around it.

In our world there is no war that has not had its basis in previous injustice of one type or another. If I believe that injustice has been done to me, I will not rectify matters by fighting with other people. Jesus made this so perfectly clear in the fifth chapter of St Matthew's Gospel: 'if someone slaps you on the right side of the cheek, turn to offer the other side also' (Matthew 5.39). What does that actually mean in fact? We learn the doctrine of Jesus further on:

> You have learnt what they were told: love your neighbour and hate your enemy but what I tell you is this: love your enemy and pray for your persecutors, only so can you be children of your Heavenly Father who makes the sun rise on good and bad alike, and sends the rain on the honest and the dishonest. If you love only those who love you, what reward can you expect? Surely the tax gatherers do as much as that. And if you greet only your brothers, what is there extraordinary about that? Even the heathen do as much. There must be no limit to your goodness as your Heavenly Father's goodness knows no bounds. (Matthew 5.43–48)

It is only when you are in that state of grace that you are no longer bound by any considerations of what is your due and what you should be getting from other people. You are now in an attitude of peace with all people and you have no more enemies at all. If there is justice in your life and in the world, then doubt and faith come close together: doubt that anything can be done by the power of the human being acting on its own; faith as the essence of love, bringing what seems impossible to fruition.

There is no harm in doubt querying physical and psychical phenomena of one type or another. If I were to doubt the veracity of many of the phenomena quoted in the Bible, in the Old Testament and the Gospels particularly, that would be no great sin. After all I am the doubter and the doubt, I am the hymn the Brahmin sings. What is important is to be open and see that many things are beyond my understanding, and I come close to them only when I can be quiet and still, and know that I know nothing.

The way towards the knowledge of God is the knowledge of complete stillness, quietness, and obliteration of egoism. But while you feel that you should be getting this, or that other people are unjust to you, or that you know the right way and other people are stupid, and you alone can treat them properly, you can cause an immense amount of trouble.

There are a number of facts about the human situation that are worth remembering. The first is that we are all children of God, the second is that we are all basically ignorant on an intellectual level and that the intellect never brings us to happiness, no matter how wonderful it may be in its own constructiveness. The third is that bodily health is a very blessed state of existence, and it comes not by doing anything but by living a proper life, a life of giving to others in concern about the well-being of the world. The fourth is that an active mind is the greatest gift that God can give us because then we can read, hear, listen, understand, and contribute on a mental level to other people. Fifthly, God shows himself moment by moment in the life that he provides, for he is above all else a living God and through his life he comes to us all and stimulates us and makes us into new and greater people. We as Christians see that life fully manifested in the life blood of Jesus himself, and from that life comes the doubt of suffering, of crucifixion, and then the marvellous revelation through resurrection which brings us to the true life.

Why did Jesus have to be crucified in order to be resurrected? Was it there merely to prove this phenomenon was necessary before we would know Jesus properly? Nobody can really answer this question categorically because it is beyond us. I think it was a part of the necessary natural history of Jesus not only in relationship to himself but also to the world. He showed that the world had to be disabused of its various follies, and when it was absolutely dark, as it was just after the crucifixion, a light could come to light up the world and bring a reality to all who lived in it. Then at last that which was dark was lit up as the Paschal candle at the time of the resurrection. Then at last all people would know the living nature of God.

To say as I have said before that our God is a living God and to quote the doctrine of the Holy Trinity is extremely stimulating. What does it really mean in the end? It means that God shows himself in the form of the greatest of all, when we have moved beyond the individual to the community. This is why a single view of God, quite excellent and certainly a part of the revealed religion as in the case of Judaism and Islam, is not quite adequate. When we see God fully, we see him full of the Spirit and the Son also, so that every part of our living universe is embraced in the constitution of God. Nothing is outside his scope when we see how he is involved in every aspect of the created universe.

If all this can be done, we begin to understand the nature of what God is telling us and then we can be at rest in our life. Therefore, the faith of Christ is bound up in the doubt of his being; not that he was not what he was, but that we can never understand the full nature of the incarnation and what it has done to the world. Then we can begin to see how much greater it is than we could possibly put into any words on a purely intellectual level. It is not a question of asking whether this did or did not happen, or whether it was really true or false; rather, that it was in all the circumstances true and that we are not in our present state of understanding capable of citing the whole mystery in the fullness of being. It is only when we realize that we know so little of the truth of creation that we can come to the knowledge of God and see how all things work together for good to them who love God (Romans 8.28). Indeed, then there is nothing that is evil or bad. Many things are unpleasant and we have to go through them as part of our growth into adults, but if we go through with strength, faith, and love – and doubt as well, let me say – we will emerge as stronger, more authentic individuals, more able to face the problems of everyday life, and come through them as decent people, full of the strength of Jesus himself.

I have said before, and I will say again as my last contribution to this thought: we are all Christs; potential Christs, perhaps, if you prefer, rather than absolute Christs at the moment, but everything that was in Jesus is in the human as well. That is why God took on a fully human form. He suffered as we did, he bore the pain that we have to bear, but he could do it perfectly as we cannot in the same way as he could. It does not matter at all. We can only do it as best we can, remembering how feeble and frail we are. Jesus was a man of immense spiritual and psychical strength and his emotional strength was amazing also. We know nothing about his physical strength; I do not visualize him myself as a man of immense physical vitality; most spiritual people are not of that type; but he was able through his life to give of himself so absolutely to others that they began to grow and enter into the full life of a human being and begin to start to live as they ought to live. Then they would say with him: I and the Father are one (John 10.30), no one comes to the Father except by me, because in me you see the fullness of the nature of God revealed bodily.

Thanks be to God.